Creating an
Independent Income in
Real Estate

Creating an
Independent Income in
Real Estate

SECOND EDITION

MACK TRAVIS

Tadorna Press

ITHACA, NEW YORK

PRAISE FOR CREATING
AN INDEPENDENT INCOME
IN REAL ESTATE

"Mack has a complete understanding of the real estate profession. He has demonstrated his ability as a teacher, both on the page and in the classroom."
—David Funk
Director of the Cornell Baker Program in Real Estate,
Cornell University

"Travis has worked in the Ithaca Community for over thirty-five years renovating burned out shells, filling vacant buildings, taking on new developments and problem properties that most people wouldn't even consider tackling. He has made a significant contribution to our city, and his book will be an inspiration to those considering entry into the real estate field."
—Thys Van Cort
Director of Planning, City of Ithaca (retired)

"Mack Travis's book will serve as an inspiration to many of our students who have entrepreneurial leanings and who are searching for their place in the job market."
—Carl Haynes
President of Tompkins Cortland
Community College (retired)

"Travis has a keen understanding of the development process and has succeeded with projects that most developers would have left undone …"

—Kevin McLaughlin
Regional Director,
Empire State Development Corporation

"Since I graduated high school, I have been interested in real estate, and being independently employed in the trade industries I was naturally familiar with Mack Travis as a local pioneer in real estate... I was also acutely aware that the trade industries, especially landscaping, are a tiresome and grueling business, where one seldom finds financial freedom.

Creating an independent income in real estate is an easy and enjoyable to read book, as if you are getting timely wisdom from a much wiser friend... This book has inspired me to think creatively about my portfolio acquisition and encouraged me to keep pressing forward even when the banks say no.

What chance does a broke landscaper have to achieve financial freedom? As I write this 7 1/2 years after opening the book, we currently have 26 rental units, and multiple other business ventures as well, many spawning from those original deals in which we had to make things work... Thank you Mack Travis, for sharing your stories and knowledge and for caring deeply about our community and encouraging us all to dare to dream."

—Caleb Scott
Landscaper, Ithaca, New York

"First, what I liked about the book was your message that with the desire and the drive anyone can get into this business. That is true. I also like your message of hard work, building trust, and taking one deal at a time. I bought my first property in 2011. One of the things I like best besides the money and building wealth is the feeling that I am making the world a better place. I fix up the apartments, give people a clean, safe, place to live, spend money at hardware stores and area business, etc. This was sort of a surprise for me, since I got started mainly for the money. I am really not that much of a people person, but I have had to get better at it, and I often enjoy it now.

My first building was two 3-family buildings on one lot. In February this year I purchased a 4-unit property. I am in the process of purchasing another six units right now."

—Daniel Hollis
Property Owner, Connecticut

TO CAROL—my partner through it all

CONTENTS

The quotes used on each Chapter Opener
page are taken from *The I Ching or Book of Changes:
The Hexagram—"Limitations."* (Copyright 1977,
Princeton University Press, Princeton NJ)

CONTENTS

ACKNOWLEDGMENTS

Many friends and associates have assisted with the creation of this book. My thanks to Holly Menino Bailey, my original editor and advisor; Carl Haynes, President of Tompkins Cortland Community College; David Funk, Director of Cornell Program in Real Estate; Thys VanCort, Director of City Planning, Ithaca, NY (Retired); Kevin McLaughlin with Empire State Development; Ron Poole with Chemung Canal Trust Company (now with M&T Bank); Paul Velleman, friend and advisor; Alan Vogel, friend and fellow developer; Chris Haine, Architect and graduate student of the Cornell Baker Program in Real Estate; Andrew Dixon and David Plaine—advisors and sounding board; Tony Sorhaindo and Della Mancuso for assistance with the revisions and second printing; to my business associates—my son, Frost Travis and his wife Kate, to my daughter and her husband, Elsa and Chris Hyde and to my wife and partner in more than just real estate, Carol Travis.

My thanks and appreciation also to the friends and family members who allowed me to tell their stories. You will meet them in the pages that follow.

PREFACE TO THE
2020 REVISED EDITION

It was mid-February 2020. My friend Tony and I had just dropped off a 90-year old friend at the Boston General Hospital for a medical consultation and were headed for Maine. Tony had helped me edit the revised version of this book, as well as my sequel to this book—*Shaping a City, Ithaca, New York: A Developer's Perspective*.

About 8:00 a.m., we rounded a corner in downtown Boston near Copley Square, and there it was, a three-story heap of rubble atop of which sat two of the largest Volvo wrecking excavators I had ever seen. Next to them were the shattered remains of what they were tearing down—a 12-14 story building.

"Now there's a problem," I exclaimed. And at the same time, we both blurted out—*"There is an opportunity!"*

While we are not going to go back through the entire text of *Creating an Independent Income in Real Estate* before publication, when you read about finding a *problem* (an old or under-utilized building, or a vacant buildable site)—of course, you are looking for the *opportunity* (to renovate, or build a new building) *within the problem*. Very soon this will become a mind-set for you.

One person's problem is another's opportunity—or it can be. *Keep your eyes open for the opportunity within the problem!*

Mack Travis

INTRODUCTION

Creating an independent income in real estate is possible. It is possible whether you have thousands of dollars in the bank to begin with, or not a penny to your name. The process begins with your desire—nothing more.

The first property is the hardest. By focusing on your desire to purchase a property and your desire to have more money, rather than on all the imagined obstacles in your way, this book will gently guide and inspire you over the initial hurdles to real estate investing. The stories here are to inspire confidence. This is not a PhD thesis, nor is it a detailed numbers book on how to analyze and maximize profit. You can find a list of some of those in Appendix C, "For Further Reading." The goal of this simple and engaging book is to inspire you in your ability to buy property, whether you have money or not, and to expose you to the basics of owning and managing income property and growing your portfolio to whatever level you desire.

You will read the stories of several of my friends and family members—how they became involved buying income properties. Some have been very successful, some have not, but the basics are here. You will read examples from my own experience buying and building a real estate portfolio over the past forty years, and you will gain the confidence that you can do it too.

Not everyone should get involved in purchasing and managing income property—but if you have been thinking about it, and it's a recurring thought, even a borderline obsession—then perhaps you should consider purchasing your first property. This book will give you the tools to begin, and if you have already begun, it will give you examples and show you the steps to further, and more complicated development.

The ones who succeed in real estate are the ones who have the Desire, the Drive, and the Discipline, these lead to Delivery—"The Four Ds." They make it happen.

Remember—with each property you purchase you are creating an increment of a lifetime income. You own it. You control it, and as long as you meet your financial obligations to lenders, no one can take it away from you. You too can create an independent income in real estate.

DESIDERATA

Go placidly amid the noise and haste,
and remember what peace there may be in silence.
As far as possible without surrender
be on good terms with all persons.
Speak your truth quietly and clearly;
and listen to others,
even the dull and the ignorant;
they too have their story.

Avoid loud and aggressive persons,
they are vexations to the spirit.
If you compare yourself with others,
you may become vain and bitter;
for always there will be greater and lesser persons than yourself.
Enjoy your achievements as well as your plans.

Keep interested in your own career, however humble;
it is a real possession in the changing fortunes of time.
Exercise caution in your business affairs;
for the world is full of trickery.
But let this not blind you to what virtue there is;
many persons strive for high ideals;
and everywhere life is full of heroism.

Be yourself.
Especially, do not feign affection.
Neither be cynical about love;
for in the face of all aridity and disenchantment
it is as perennial as the grass.

Take kindly the counsel of the years,
gracefully surrendering the things of youth.
Nurture strength of spirit to shield you in sudden misfortune.
But do not distress yourself with dark imaginings.
Many fears are born of fatigue and loneliness.
Beyond a wholesome discipline,
be gentle with yourself.

You are a child of the universe,
no less than the trees and the stars;
you have a right to be here.
And whether or not it is clear to you,
no doubt the universe is unfolding as it should.

Therefore be at peace with God,
whatever you conceive Him to be,
and whatever your labors and aspirations,
in the noisy confusion of life keep peace with your soul.

With all its sham, drudgery, and broken dreams,
it is still a beautiful world.
Be cheerful.
Strive to be happy.

—Written in 1927 by
Max Ehrmann 1872-1945

CHAPTER 1

YOU CAN DO IT:
My Own Story and the Tools You Will Need

Unlimited possibilities are not
suited to man; if they existed, his life would
dissolve in the boundless.

Not everyone should get involved in purchasing and managing income property. You will need some basic skills—to be able to add and subtract; the ability to talk to people; to be able to stick with a project, and to persevere through the ups and downs each project will go through. And at whatever level you enter this field, you will need the driving desire to make your projects succeed. While it is not for everyone, if you have those basic skills, there is no doubt you can succeed in this field.

My own career in real estate began in New York City. In 1968, I net-leased a four-story brownstone on West 82nd Street in Manhattan. It was a row house, vacant, with rats and musty rooms and an open stairwell connecting each floor. It had been someone's lovely mansion in by-gone days. Now it was little more than a vacant flop house in an area of the City that my friends dubbed the "armpit" of New York. The rent for the whole building was $275 a month.

It took four months to clean, paint, and generally spruce up the building to make it habitable. The entire top floor rented to a friend. My wife and I, with our daughter and infant son, lived on the second and third floor, and other friends took the two apartments on the first floor. Adding up all the income from the apartments, we received enough money to pay the net lease for the building, pay the heat and water bill, and live rent-free with eight rooms in the middle of Manhattan—not a bad deal. The owner offered to sell me the entire building for $40,000, but that was an unattainable fortune for me in 1968.

I had gone to New York to be an actor, but after six months of auditions and part-time typing jobs, it was clear that even having been a big star in college theater and graduate school and even having earned my Actor's Equity card in several seasons of summer stock theater—in New York City this "actor" was just a little speck of dew. It was no way for me to make a living. After taking a quick course at the New York Institute of Photography and learning how to be an assistant cameraman, I freelanced making industrial and sales films for small firms.

We lived in New York City for another two years and eventually my wife and I separated. I moved on to Ithaca, New York, taking a job at Ithaca College teaching film production for a salary of $8,000 a year, $666 a month. My wife and children moved to Georgia, where she had taken a teaching job. Every month, half my salary went to my wife and children. It didn't take long for me to realize that my income was far exceeded by my outgo, and it was either sell shoes on Saturdays to augment my meager income or buy an income property and see if there was a way to make ends meet.

I had absolutely no money and thought back to New

York City. It suddenly made sense to begin looking at houses. There was a small white house next to the largest waterfall in Ithaca. It belonged to a friend of mine. The house was tiny, but maybe he would sell it for very little and it could be rented out. The problem: my friend didn't want to sell. No matter how often I asked him to consider it, he was not ready to sell—in the future maybe, but not now—and I needed money now!

Out of the blue, one of my coworkers at the college said he would sell me his house downtown. He had been trying to sell it for years so that he could move to California and had lowered the price repeatedly. Finally, he said to me, "You take over my payments, and it's yours!" He was offering me his house basically for free, but even at that it was a huge step. It was agony for me trying to decide whether or not to go ahead with it. Could I make the payments? What happens if the roof leaks? What happens if the plumbing breaks? What happens if it doesn't rent? In spite of my fears, I finally took the plunge. My first house was going to close for $11,000— no money down! I went to the closing using my friend's attorney, as I couldn't afford one of my own. At the closing his attorney told me $500 was required for the closing costs. That was a surprise. Excusing myself, I ran to the bank, maxed out my only credit card and went back to the attorney's office with the cash. That was the true beginning of my real estate career—I now owned my first piece of property.

Working evenings and weekends and scavenging for materials, I was able to rearrange the entrance to the upstairs, add a bathroom and second kitchen, and turn the single-family house into a two-family house. It rented quickly and brought in $100 a month above expenses. It was almost enough to make ends meet. I figured by purchasing and renovating ten houses and making $100 a month each, I could retire.

It didn't work out quite that way. Looking back now, forty years later, on the events that followed borrowing, purchasing, renovating and eventually developing a number of projects from the ground up has resulted in holdings in real estate worth multiple millions of dollars. However, whatever one's current level of wealth, whatever one's current level of accomplishment or success, it is important to keep one's perspective. As stated in one of my favorite poems, *Desiderata*, "If you compare yourself with others, you may become vain or bitter, for always there will be greater or lesser persons than yourself."

There will always be those with larger holdings, more success, more wealth, and there will always be those with smaller holdings, less wealth, less success. The important thing is to start from where you are; start with what you want.

Over the years, I have been invited to lecture in graduate programs for both the Cornell Hotel School and the Cornell Baker Program in Real Estate. Although many of the students in these programs will become the billionaire owners and real estate managers of the future, and many are from families who already own significant real estate portfolios, my role has been to present the position of the local, small-town real estate owner and developer.

The basic principles and skills for growth in real estate are the same whether you aspire to the billionaire status, or whether you are purchasing your very first single-family or duplex house. You still need to be able to add and subtract, to be able to talk to people, and to persevere through the ups and downs of each project, and you still need to have a driving desire to make each project succeed. It didn't take more than the first project or two for me realize that I had the ability and the desire to *create an independent income in real estate*. If you are drawn to it, you can too.

CHAPTER 2

THE PLAYERS:
The People I Have Taught

---

*To become strong, a man's life
needs the limitations ordained by duty
and voluntarily accepted.*

Recently, a local bank agreed to lend us $400,000. My son had set the process in motion for us to secure a subsidized rate of 3% on a loan from our local public utility to install new boilers and implement energy-efficiency measures in three of our apartment complexes. He had taken off on vacation with his wife and one-year-old son, and I was sitting in his stead, in the office of the young commercial lender, signing pages of documents guaranteeing repayment of this unsecured loan. Midway through the process, the loan officer paused and asked if he could talk to me about real estate. I assured him that there was nothing I liked better than to talk about real estate.

"What should I do to get started?" he asked. "I've got a great salary at the bank, a great pension. I often work long hours, but it is only really required that I work nine to five. I can go home at five and spend time with my one-and-a-half-year-old son. My wife is a teacher; she gets home at three o'clock every day. Between us we make over $150,000 a year. We have a great lifestyle. But I want more. I thought real estate might be a good way to plan for retirement. I've seen what you have created. I don't want to take up your time, but could I take you to lunch sometime and talk with you about it?"

"Certainly. I'll make you a deal. Right now, I'm advising five people in their real estate careers, each one is at a different stage in the process. Lately, I've been thinking a lot about how to pass on my knowledge, and if you will ask me your questions, I will give you my answers." He seemed satisfied with our arrangement. We finished signing the documents and he handed over a bank check for the $400,000. We agreed to meet in the near future.

Back at my office that afternoon, there was a third phone call in as many weeks from a friend in California. We had met during a ten-day hiking and camping trip in the Sierra Nevadas last summer. During the trip, he had found out about my background investing in income property for forty years, and began plying me with questions about how he could get involved. He was forty-nine years old and had developed and owned a motorcycle racing company. He and his riders had raced for sixteen years, and they had won as many national championships. He told me of his career—building his business, hiring racers, and roaring around the nation's motorcycle racetracks at 170 miles an hour, and I told him of mine—starting with a single-family house and gradually building a portfolio of apartments, offices, retail buildings, and medical offices in upstate New York. We were struck by the similarity of our paths—intense focus, intense excitement, and intense satisfaction from the results. But he was older now and ready to change careers. He had thought of starting a series of Jiffy

Lube franchises, but after our many hours of conversation at that altitude of twelve thousand feet in the High Sierras, he was ready to begin a career in real estate acquisition. I agreed to assist him, and he had called me regularly to tell me of his progress raising equity and researching properties, as well as to get my direction and advice.

The weekend before, I had driven to North Carolina to spend a few days with my niece and her husband, who in their late twenties had already finished the purchase and renovation of their second thirty-unit apartment complex. Following my advice along the way, they had been able to purchase both projects with no money down, and they were in the process of choosing their next project. They had a number of terrific opportunities in a small town adjacent to the Research Triangle in North Carolina, and they wanted my advice on which projects to focus on.

As we drove around town looking at a dozen different vacant buildings, all possibilities for purchase with little or no cash, all vacant and run-down—they admitted to me their heads were spinning. Where should they start? Which project should they begin with? With their two successes in the downtown in as many years, people were coming out of the woodwork to ask them to purchase their properties. Even the city planner and the city manager were offering them for free, a prime site the city owned in the heart of this sad and neglected downtown, if they would only develop a project.

I spent an extra day with them to help them focus in on which projects could be negotiated to a reasonable purchase price, would be the least risky, had the most potential for profit, and would be of the most benefit to the community.

We met with a consultant who the city had hired to do a master plan—envisioning how the city could grow over the next twenty years, which projects would have the most impact, and how to attract developers to their downtown.

My niece and her husband were on a roll, and they asked me to stay yet one more day for a meeting they had arranged with the city manager, city planner, and city development officer. The purpose of the meeting would be to discuss their plans for mixed-use development which would house a co-op grocery store, offices, and sixty residential units. Already, at their young age, and with their two successfully completed projects, they had established credibility and an exceptional track record. They were now preparing to move ahead on an $8 million project in their downtown, undaunted by the fact that they had little or no cash. They had a vision and a desire. The money for the projects, they were confident from their accumulated experience—would come.

During my time in North Carolina, I shuttled back and forth between my niece and her husband in one town, and my sister and her husband in another. Over twenty or so years, my sister and her husband had purchased twenty student-rental properties around their local university. He was a very successful insurance broker, she a local artist and community volunteer. Although they had been purchasing and managing rental units over twenty years, neither of them really understood bookkeeping. My sister had been keeping the books as best she could, and in reviewing them, it was obvious they had been recording tenant security deposits on the apartments as income and using the money for expenses—not a good idea, because each year they had had to refinance a property to repay last year's security deposits back to the tenants. They had listened to my warning a year ago that their ability to continually borrow against their equity in the properties would cease at some point, and they would feel the pinch. We spent several late nights together working on budgets for each property, budgets that would set aside the security deposits in an escrow account as they received them and put each property on its own financial footing. Though they are both smart people, it was necessary to drill into them the need to be realistic with their bookkeeping. I think they finally got it.

Meanwhile, my second wife, Carol, was in Florida visiting her daughter and husband, and their newly arrived baby daughter. Carol's daughter worked for the City of Sarasota, and her husband, although licensed as a building contractor, was currently out of work and had been unable to find a job. Together they owned two adjacent five-acre sites some forty miles from Sarasota, one with a house, a barn, and several outbuildings, the other with a mobile home. They had experience renting the mobile home to various relatives and friends, but they were often more big-hearted than business-minded when it came time to collect the rent. Over the years, we had tried to interest them in purchasing additional rental property, but questions always came up: "What if we can't pay the mortgage? What if the units don't rent? What then? What then?" They didn't feel comfortable handling the risk. And besides, they were sure they couldn't raise the money for a down payment.

Carol was enjoying her granddaughter and had cooked and cleaned to give the parents a break with the new baby.

While there, she had also driven our son-in-law around to look at properties for sale. They had found several houses in foreclosure and an eight-unit apartment building that seemed like a possibility. Perhaps with the arrival of the baby, his current unemployment, and the experience they had with renting and managing the rental unit on their property, they would be ready to branch out. They liked the idea of the security and additional income a rental property might bring, but they lacked the skill and confidence, and the down payment to acquire it—or so they thought.

They were facing the same dilemma that I had faced with my first property almost forty years ago. They were driven by the need to make more money, but they feared failure if they tried investing in real estate. We didn't know yet if they would choose to go to work for someone else, or if they would venture out on their own.

My young banker friend with whom I had agreed to exchange questions and answers about real estate investing had the right idea—find out all you can about a subject, and the fear goes away, or at least it dissipates enough to allow you to move forward if you choose to, or to find another way if you decide real estate isn't the path for you. This was certainly what my stepdaughter and her husband needed to do.

Leaving North Carolina to drive back home to upstate New York, I phoned the widow of a former investor of mine who lived in Frederick, Maryland. And yes, she would be available to see me, and yes, she would love to have dinner with me that night at her assisted-living facility. Her husband had invested in a twenty-unit property with me in the mid-1980s. My son and I had refinanced the property, and at her request we had purchased her interest in it earlier in the fall. She was one of a dozen and a half people I had "supported" around the country—people who had sold me property and had personally lent me the money that enabled me to buy the property from them and pay them back over time. They had "taken back paper" as it is referred to in real estate jargon. "Taking back paper" is another term for "owner financing" on all or a portion of the sales price. The seller may be willing to carry a mortgage on the property—a first mortgage if they are lending you the full amount of the purchase price, or more likely a second mortgage behind the bank's first, thereby enabling you to buy the property with little or no cash of your own.

Some had even invested with me as partners. This had given me the resources to grow our real estate business. Whenever possible, I make it a point to call on these participants in my real estate ventures for a little face time. In my experience, face time, and a check on the same day each month make for a strong and happy bond between me and my investors.

CHAPTER 3

THE PROCESS:
Decide What You Want, Trust Your Desires

---

*The individual attains significance as a
free spirit by surrounding himself with these limitations
and determining for himself what his duty is.*

Fear of the unknown can paralyze us. We can stop all action
out of fear. Or we can get ourselves moving out of fear—fear
of annihilation, fear of failure, fear of poverty. It is our choice
to quiver in the corner, or to venture out to find the solution.

Thirty years ago, a friend gave me a small book called *It
Works*. It was little more than a pamphlet of twenty-six pages,
first published in 1926, quaint in its wording but timeless in
its advice.

The basic premise is simple, but it is profound: Decide
what you want. Write it down. Read your list daily, several times. Don't worry about how it works. It promises that
whatever you write down on your list of true desires and focus on several times a day, whatever it is you want, will come
to you. It's that simple.

In my experience, it doesn't mean you just make your
list and then sit back, relax and do nothing. It does mean
that once you know what you want and write it down, the
pathways begin to open up. You begin to realize where you
should expend your effort, and you clearly understand the

decisions you need to make to realize your desires. Once you write down and know exactly *what you want* and continue to *review your list daily*, these things begin to come to you in an efficient, reliable, and remarkably effortless way.

We already use this technique unconsciously on some level. We have survived to this point. Very likely we have enough to eat, and clothes to wear; we have some place to live; we have a livelihood of some sort, and we may have friends and maybe even love in our life. Perhaps it has just happened to us. If we're fortunate, our parents have set the process in motion for us. They have cared for us and loved us enough to get us launched. Now we are on our own, and it is up to us. We want things. We need things. We need love and affection. And although we may not be consciously aware of it, or may not have objectively realized it, *desire* is at the basis of what we have, who we are, how we earn our livelihood. At some point we have the desire to eat, the desire to live where we are, the desire to be with the person we are with, or not.

We often are content to just let things happen to us. We want things, and we get them, but we may not take a truly active approach in determining a satisfactory outcome. Or perhaps we have taken an active role in determining who we are, what we do, where we live, who we are with. In either case, the principle in this little book *It Works*—actively determining what you want and writing it down (i.e., attention, focus and intention)—will speed you on your way.

One of the personal roadblocks I have had to confront is the notion that desires are somehow bad. That it is wrong to desire things for oneself. It is somehow sinful to desire, or even, as my Buddhist friends point out, desire is the cause of all suffering. How could this be correct? If we don't desire anything, we don't suffer? No. No. No. If we don't desire something, we will never get it. It's that simple. We must desire. We cannot live without desire.

However, it is important to understand that it is not the desire itself that causes stress and suffering, but rather, it is the inability to fulfill the desire that leads to stress and suffering—fulfilled desires lead to a sense of accomplishment and contentment. It is possible to desire without attachment to the outcome. That is the secret. Desire something. Focus on it. Know that it will come to you, but don't worry it to death. Let it come in its own time, in its own way. Desires lead to plans. Plans lead to action. Action leads to results. Results lead to fulfillment and satisfaction. Trying to give up desires in order to avoid pain and disappointment will likely lead to a flat and unproductive life. Demanding that life fulfill our desires will indeed lead to disappointment and suffering but having the desires and holding them gently in our minds and hearts—doing our work while holding them gently as part of our being, will without a doubt, lead to success and fulfillment.

How do you know if your desires are correct for you? Don't worry about it. Write them down. You will gradually know which ones are real for you and which are not. Some will drop away as you revise your list. New ones will occur to you. As you get results, you will gain confidence in the process.

Should my young banker friend get involved in real estate? My advice would be for him to look at it. Ask his questions. If he continues to be drawn to it after finding out what it entails, perhaps he should. Perhaps you should. You will have to decide if your security and financial well-being will be better served by putting energy into your current job or diversifying into a second field. Will the extra hours you will invariably spend finding, analyzing, purchasing, and managing an income property produce more money and security for you and your family than focusing those hours on the field you are currently in? Do you like what you do now? Think about it. Think about what you truly want. Make that list. Examine it daily and continue to refine it over a period of time. Trust yourself. You will come to know what the right direction is for you.

People pay one another for performing a service. We can serve each other by providing bank loans, growing crops, educating our children, repairing a car, taking a customer's money as a grocery clerk. The only reason people will pay us is that we are giving them something they want or need. It is no different in the real estate field. We all need a place to live, a place to work, a place to vacation or spend free time. That place can be any type of structure: a house, shop, office, or a skyscraper. For any structure, you can be assured someone conceived of it, designed it, financed it, built it, perhaps renovated it, and now manages it—whether it is your home, the place you work or shop, the place where you go for your medical treatment, or where you live in your old age. Someone literally desired that structure into being. And someone is paying to live in it, rent it, own it, and maintain it, because it fulfills a service to themselves and others. There is no inherent value in bricks and mortar.

A structure that performs no service to other people is

worthless. A person who performs no service to other people, does not provide someone, somewhere, with what they
want, usually does not realize their income potential, nor do
they find much satisfaction in life. You will find that getting
in touch with your core desires will set you on the path of
performing the greatest service, first to yourself, and thereby
to others. As you perform the service you have chosen, you
will invariably reap the rewards you desire.

As you write down your desires, you will find that your
fear of the unknown will disappear. Focus on yourself, what
you truly want. *Write down what you want.* Fear of not getting it will shrink to the size of a small pea in the corner of
the room. Your desires will instead fill the room. And as you
focus gently on your desires, the solutions will begin to appear. Organization and focus, a plan of action—will supplant
the fear of inaction and not knowing. Desires, solutions, a
plan of action will fill the room. Focus on your desires.

No one can take your desires away from you. Desires are
at the basis of all we do. They are what we want. They are
what we will get in life. They are in large part, who we are.
How big can you think? How big can you desire? I am fond
of saying, "Desires are God-given." Trust them. They are
yours. Trust yourself. Over the years I have ordered hundreds
of copies of *It Works* for friends and students. You can order
it online from DeVorss Publications, at www.devorss.com.

CHAPTER 4

GETTING STARTED:
Problems Equal Opportunites

---

*When the time has come
for action, the moment must
be quickly seized.*

What questions do you need to ask and to answer for yourself in order to move forward? For a moment, imagine there is not one single obstacle to keep you from purchasing an income property. Is this something you really desire to do? Can you do it? What are the tools and the mind-set you need to do it? How can you be sure it will be successful and not bring you down financially? There are no obstacles, only opportunities.

You've heard that location is the primary consideration when purchasing property, usually repeated three times: "Location, location, location is the most important thing to consider when purchasing an income property." That may be true but add one thing further to the list. *Your own location* is one of the most important things to consider. Are you living where you think you want to remain for a while? Are you settled enough to stay there for two years? It will probably take you that long to find your first piece of property, figure out how to purchase it, fix it up, rent it, and either refinance it, sell it, or assimilate it into your growing portfolio. It is easier to do this when you can drive five or ten minutes to work on it, show it, and manage it. It will take some time to become successful. Make it easy on yourself with the first one. Buy something close by, where you know the neighborhood. Furthermore, it will be difficult to convince a banker or seller to lend you money to purchase your first project if you are still living out of the back of your car.

Let's continue to assume there are no insurmountable obstacles, and you have a growing desire to purchase your first property. You have heard of many people creating an independent income in real estate. Thousands of people have done just that. Why not you?

Your first question: I don't have any money, how can I do it without money? At this point we are not worrying about the money. Money is just a tool. If you need a hammer, you go out and find one. You may find it in a closet. You may save a little to purchase one. You may go out and borrow one from a friend or a passerby. *Money is just a tool. Don't worry about the money.* There's a lot of money out there. The main thing you need at this point is the desire. You're going to think about it for a while. Is this something you really, really want to look into? If it is, let's go on to the next question.

How do I get started? If you were going to buy a car or a lawnmower, or you were new in town and wanted to know the best grocery store or pharmacy, how would you go about it? You'd check around with your friends, you'd listen to their experiences about what was the best brand, the best deal, the best place to shop. You'd read the paper, or go online, and see what the ads and reviews say. You'd do a little research before going shopping. It's not that different shopping for your first income property.

Drive around. Walk around. Find a neighborhood you like. Are there "For-Sale" signs in the front yards? Talk to your friends. Do they know of any houses for sale? Pick up your local paper and read the ads in the real estate section; check out Zillow or other online real estate listings; look for properties "For Sale by Owner"—occasionally you will find one of these. Become familiar with the housing market in your area. Call a real estate broker and ask if they have any income properties for sale. They will ask what you are looking for—what size, what price range? Tell them two to four units for starters, or if you are really ambitious, say eight to ten units. As far as price, tell them you are looking for the "right deal." Once you start to network and see what is available, you will have a better idea of the possibilities in your area.

Narrow down the possibilities. Call the owner or a broker. Go to look at the first property. Remember, at this point, money is not an obstacle. And remember, the first property is the hardest one to buy! It costs nothing to look, and it will be the beginning of your education into the world of real estate. *Just by looking*, you will have taken the first step toward creating an independent income in real estate.

What do you look for? You are getting familiar with the market in your area. You are looking for an opportunity to purchase a property from someone who is motivated to sell. My first property was a single-family house. The seller wanted to leave town quickly, and he simply let me take over his payments. That was a no-brainer. Someone in your town may want out of their property badly enough to sell it to you at a deep discount, let you take over the payments, or possibly lend you the money you need for a down payment. You are looking for a deal. Do not be embarrassed or afraid to ask for the moon; ask, "Are you willing to take back paper?" Figure out what you want and ask for it. If you have already saved some money for a down payment, that will open up even more possibilities.

How will you know when you have found the right property? Owning property is a numbers game. Each income property will have an income stream. You will ask the seller for a rent roll, a list of each unit and what the tenants pay monthly. You will also ask the seller for an accounting of expenses. A renter pays the rent and has little else to worry about other than perhaps a trash expense, parking fee, and an electric or gas bill, depending on how the property is set up. A property owner has to pay for maintenance, management, taxes, insurance, water/sewer, and utilities for the common areas, if not also the units. Owners must pay for landscaping, snow removal if applicable, and improvements and upkeep of the property including roofs, heating and air conditioning (HVAC), repainting, repaving—the list goes on. Beyond that, the owner must pay for the debt service. The important thing is that once you have added up all of the expenses for a property, the income must exceed the outgo.

The following income and expense template will give you an idea of how to analyze the income and expense for a property. It contains a lot of information and assumptions that may not be clear to you at this point, but they are the essential categories that go into any property analysis.

INCOME-EXPENSE TEMPLATE			
Assumptions	**Budget Year**	**Monthly**	**Annually**
INCOME			
4 one-bedroom apartments @ $650	Rent	$2,600	$31,200
Assume 5% vacancy	Vacancy	($130)	($1,560)
None Planned	Late Fee	$0	$0
$5/pet/month; say 2 pets	Pet Fee	$10	$120
$10/month/unit	Trash/Recycling Fee	$40	$480
4 spaces @ $25/month	Parking Income	$100	$1,200
	Total Income	**$2,620**	**$31,440**
	EXPENSES		
	MAINTENANCE		
$50/unit/month	Labor	$200	$2,400
$50/unit/month	Materials/Supplies	$200	$2,400
	Total Maintenance	**$400**	**$4,800**
	MANAGEMENT		
Estimate	Advertising	$25	$300
None Planned	Legal	$0	$0
Once a year fee	Accounting	$25	$300
5% of Total Income	Management Fee	$131	$1,572
	Total Management	**$181**	**$2,172**

Assumptions	Budget Year	Monthly	Annually
	INSURANCE		
Estimate 2.5% of income	Property/Liability	**$66**	**$786**
Depends on property set up	**UTILITIES**		
Estimate $10/unit/month	Water & Sewer	$40	$480
Common Areas only (Tenant pays for unit)	Electricity	$25	$300
Owner pays heat	Gas Utility	$100	$1,200
Tenant Pays	Trash Removal	$40	$480
	Total Utilities	**$205**	**$2,460**
Will depend on local tax rates & billing policies	**TAXES**		
Avegrage per month billed twice a year	City Property Taxes	$175	$2,100
Avegrage per month billed once a year	School Property Taxes	$242	$2,900
Avegrage per month billed twice a year	County Property Taxes	$ 83	$1,000
	Total Taxes	**$500**	**$6,000**
1st Mortgage - $112,000 @ 6% for 25 yrs	1st Mortgage: Principal & Interest	$722	$8,664
Appliances, carpet, roof, etc. escrow account	Major Improvements	$200	$2,400
	TOTAL EXPENSES	**$2,274**	**$27,282**
	CASH FLOW	**$347**	**$4,158**

This Income-Expense analysis will become more understandable to you as we look at other deals.

Don't despair if the numbers don't work on the first pass. They seldom do. What can you do to increase income? Will the market support an increase in rents? You will know that from your research on rents in your area. Can you charge for parking where they did not charge for that before? Can you charge a trash fee of $10 to $15 per unit per month? It will probably be necessary to negotiate the purchase price. You should go to at least two local banks and see which one will give you the best rate and terms. The cost of each $10,000 of a loan at 6% paid off, or "amortized," over twenty years is $71.64 per month. At 7%, the cost is $77.53 per month; the difference between 6% and 7% on every $10,000 is $5.89 per month. That may not seem like much but multiply that by the amount you will need to borrow, and it will add up.

Changing the term of the same loan to twenty-five years lowers the monthly payment to $64.43 and $70.68, respectively; thirty years changes the monthly amount on $10,000 to $59.96 and $66.53. It pays to shop for the financing as well as for the right piece of property.

What can you do yourself? Can you save a management fee of 5% to 10% of gross rents by collecting the rents and taking the maintenance calls yourself? Can you save money by cutting the lawn, and making minor repairs? Do you have evenings and weekends free to look after your property? The numbers can change quickly for the better, the more you can do yourself. And that is money in your pocket.

At this point you have researched your market area. You have found a property or maybe several that appeal you. You have asked the seller for an accounting of the income and expenses. You have run a basic analysis of the numbers. You have adjusted the numbers to what the property might produce in income, and cost in expenses, if you were to manage and maintain the property based on your available time and skill level.

However, you may suddenly convince yourself that this is not a good time to buy—all the good properties are taken; the market is too up; the market is too down—my advice is to not listen to your fears, your friends, or a newscaster's analysis of the state of the market. Focus fully on your desire to own an income property and keep looking until you find the deal that is right for you.

The temptation is to look for the biggest, fanciest, most well-maintained properties in your area. My approach has always been to *look for a problem*. It doesn't have to be as dramatic as the Boston demolition example mentioned in the preface to this, the second edition, but if you can find a property that is partially vacant, run-down, with low rents, even one that is burned out and empty, this may be the property for you. *Buying a property at the top of the market leaves you little room to grow.* The only way to go is up by the rate of inflation or by the rate of appreciation of the market in your area. If you can find a property that is 25% vacant, and you can identify why it is vacant and can solve the problem, you will have immediately increased the value of your property by 25% or more.

CHAPTER 5

MIKE'S STORY:
Finding the Property, Analyzing the Deal

---

*It is a good thing to hesitate so
long as the time for action has not come,
but no longer.*

Pine Level, Florida, is about as flat as land can get. Carol and I arrived at the Fort Myers Airport on the 10:55 p.m. flight from Syracuse. We drove through the dark, and pouring rain for an hour to our daughter Livy's house. Carol had been here just weeks earlier, and now we had both come to spend a few days with our new granddaughter, who was nearly two months old, and to talk with Livy and our son-in-law Mike, about real estate investing.

The next morning, we walked around their five-acre spread with Mike, feeding the geese, the goats, and Toby, their boisterous pony. Their half-acre pond was teeming with turtles and pin-tail ducks that came and went. Mike was thirty-eight years old, had his contractor's license, and had worked for the past several years for his brother-in-law, building houses within a several hours' drive of their home. At this point, in the winter of 2008, the housing market in Florida had collapsed. The financial markets worldwide were in disarray, and credit had virtually dried up, at least for the major national banks.

Over the past several weeks at home, I had spoken with three local community banks, and they said they were as secure as they had ever been, still lending money. The rates were higher than they had been—up to 7% from 6%, where they had hovered for the past five or six years. The local banks, however, were conservative and had not gotten involved in the mortgage-backed securities market, as had become the rage and now the bane of the Wall Street lenders. Loose lending practices and subprime mortgages now plagued the credit markets worldwide as people who had borrowed way beyond their means defaulted on their loans as the interest-only periods ended and payments suddenly mushroomed to include principal, and sometimes a higher interest rate. The banks that had stuck to their conservative ways and held their own loans were still lending, at least in our area in upstate New York.

That afternoon, sitting around in their living room we began our real estate conversation. Mike began telling us about the properties he had driven by and made calls about in nearby Arcadia An eight-unit building he and Carol had looked at several weeks ago had just sold. Another two-family had also just sold. A large two-story house with four bedrooms and two baths, one that he had really been attracted to, had just sold for $17,000. He had a friend whose father was getting a divorce and had to sell his four four-unit properties in Port Charlotte, about an hour's drive from Pine Level. There seemed to be properties available, but Mike felt he had missed them, and his friend hadn't returned his call about the Port Charlotte property; besides, he said, the credit markets had dried up.

Mike seemed discouraged and unable to get over the immense hurdle of the unknown. He told me about his background, of having waited tables for a few years; worked as a laborer in construction, and after he and Livy were married, he had gotten a degree in computer science and worked in an office for a while. He tired of that and decided to become a contractor. He studied and received his contractor's license and had been working for the past five years building houses, laying tile, doing masonry and carpentry, only now there was no work and they had a new baby. Livy worked for the City of Sarasota and was out on maternity leave; she would continue to receive a paycheck for ten weeks. They had refinanced their house and had some money saved that could carry them for a few months while he looked for work.

I asked him what his ideal job would be. He knew he didn't enjoy working in an office. He liked being outdoors, working with his hands. He was good at supervising, and he enjoyed construction. He and Livy had renovated a mobile home next to their house, adding a large, screened-in porch. They now rented it out. Mike had entirely renovated their own home, opening up walls and installing new flooring. He was experienced and handy.

Based on what he said, Mike had an ideal background for owning rental property. He listened while I explained the basic principles I had developed over my forty years of investing in real estate. The only reason people pay us for anything, is because we provide them with something they want. We give them goods or services, and they part with their money. Owning and managing income property is a service industry.

My own strategy evolved after buying and renovating several houses in Ithaca. I had looked around and seen that the housing stock was run-down. People were being rented junk to live in, particularly the student renters, and they took it, for there was no other choice. I had realized that adopting an approach of providing quality housing would set my properties apart from the rest, keep them full and give me the satisfaction of providing high-quality, good service. By providing good service and good value, I was confident the money would come, and it had!

Mike listened, but then he told me what he had told Carol several weeks ago—he had no way to raise a down payment. He and Livy would like to own an income property; they had watched what we had done; they had watched what my niece Wellsley and her husband Matt had done in North Carolina, but they still couldn't see how they could raise the money needed to put down for the purchase of an income property.

"Listen, Mike," I finally said, "don't worry about the money. The main thing you need is the intention. Set yourself a goal of owning an income property. As you move forward, the way will open up for you. The money will appear. All you need is the intention. Don't worry about the down payment. A way to buy the house will open up for you."

I knew that in this instance, we could help them with the down payment. All he needed was to decide he wanted to do this. But it had to come from him—from inside.

Mike listened as I gave him some examples of buying a property with little more than the desire to do so—my first house in Ithaca, where my buddy simply wanted out. He told me he would sell it; just take over the payments. I did, and it was a success.

My sister and her husband in North Carolina had bought seventeen houses over the years: They would find a seller, usually older people who had lived in their homes for many years and had paid off their bank mortgage. They would negotiate a purchase price for the house, and then continue the negotiation by asking the seller to lend them the money which the bank would require for a down payment—usually anywhere between 20-25% of the purchase price. The bank would lend the balance to my sister and her husband in a "first mortgage" using the seller's house as "security" to assure the mortgage would be repaid. This meant that the seller would receive 75-80% of the purchase price in cash, and the balance in the form of regular monthly payments, usually over a period of 10 to 20 years.

The seller would agree to lend them the down payment in the form of a "second mortgage" also secured by the house i.e., the seller would be "subordinating" this second mortgage, to the bank's first mortgage.

I asked Mike if he knew what subordinate meant. He said he had a general idea, so I spelled it out: in the event the property is foreclosed (i.e., the bank has to take it back should my sister and her husband not make their payments), the seller has a choice—they can take over the monthly payments and reclaim their property from the bank, or they can simply let it go and lose their subordinated second mortgage, but at least they have the cash they received at the sale. Mike understood that.

The effect on the seller when they subordinate to the

bank financing, is that they get cash at the closing (the first mortgage money from the bank), plus they receive an income stream of the monthly payments on the second mortgage from my sister and her husband, which had essentially covered the down payment—the cash the seller might have wanted up front. They would then rent the property for enough income to cover all the operating expenses, plus the debt service on the first mortgage with the bank and the second mortgage with the seller, plus have some left over for themselves.

I explained that this process is called "seller financing" and that it is a very common way to buy property. The benefit to the buyer is that they own the property, and the income stream from the property, without having to put any of their own money up front. However, the buyer may have to invest some "sweat equity," since they typically will need to renovate the house to increase income. They often will rearrange the rooms to maximize bedrooms or convert a basement or an attic into an additional apartment, but they own the property with no cash down payment. My sister and her husband have bought seventeen houses using this technique.

Mike heard another example of how my niece and her husband, also in North Carolina, had the desire to create an independent income in real estate. They had watched her parents succeed. They both had college degrees and had been trained and worked as Emergency Medical Technicians (EMTs). They had "taking care of people" in their blood, but they also had huge ideas about what they wanted to do. The first property they looked at was a 275,000 square-foot factory in Mebane, North Carolina. They had visions of renovating it into housing and shops in this little town and had asked my son and me to come down and advise them. We toured the building in Mebane and then visited several old brick tobacco warehouses in Durham and Chapel Hill that had been renovated by developers into incredible complexes of housing and shops.

We ran the numbers for Wellsley and Matt on their proposed Mebane development and figured they had a $20 million project on their hands. We suggested that for their first project, they might want to consider something a bit smaller, more like two or three, or maybe twenty units at the most. At first, they were disappointed but as they confronted the numbers, the complexity of the project, and the significant amount of equity they would have to raise, the reality of the situation began to set in. They could dream, but maybe not that big on their first project.

Mike was interested—it wasn't but a few months later that Wellsley and Matt had called me about another project they were considering. They had found a twenty-unit apartment complex close to Chapel Hill, where they lived. It was built in the 1920s, and although mostly rented, it was rundown and neglected. The tenants, they said, were a reflection of the building.

A young couple had purchased the building out of foreclosure and had tried unsuccessfully to renovate it. Now, they wanted to sell it for $650,000. They settled on $500,000 and agreed to take $50,000 back as a second mortgage. Wellsley and Matt had analyzed the numbers. If the bank would lend enough money for renovations and allow the seller's second mortgage, they would be able to buy it, renovate it, and pay themselves a salary for running the renovation job. In essence they would own the property with no cash down.

Mike listened. He was beginning to become intrigued with the possibility that he too could find the right property and somehow own it. My own strategy had evolved as I had found and renovated my second and third houses, always looking for a problem building. Gradually it had dawned on me that what I wanted was to buy run-down, neglected properties *that offered a problem which, properly solved, offered an opportunity to increase my income dramatically by correcting the problem*—renovating them and creating an immediate increase in their value.

This became my strategy. I would buy only properties with a problem, in good locations, with seller financing when possible, and negotiate with a bank to lend an amount based on the value of the property when fully renovated and rented (known as the "as-built" value.) Buying a property with a problem usually meant it could be purchased for no money down, since the seller was often very ready to sell. And by solving the problem—whether it was vacancy, layout, fire damage—the value could be dramatically increased beyond the original purchase price. I could own a property without having to come up with a down payment and by renovating it, I would offer only quality housing for rent.

Mike was beginning to get excited. He realized he had the skills to do this. In fact, his hands-on contracting skills were way beyond mine. The question now was the Florida real estate market. Mike told me that it was in the tank. Prices had come down. He told me of several houses he had worked on that had sat vacant for three years. The contractor involved had originally marketed them at $750,000, and now the banks were offering them at $200,000— "Anything to get them off their hands," Mike said.

Mike's excitement was contagious. This sounded like it might have the makings of a great opportunity for him. There was certainly risk, but if he could buy in a down market, that would be ideal, as long as the market came back. He said he thought it would, that it was only a matter of time.

We agreed to go into town so that he could show me the properties he had found. It took us only a few minutes to drive into Arcadia, past the flat open fields with Black Angus cattle with their attendant swarms of white cattle egrets perching on their backs and pecking along after them on the ground. On the outskirts of town, we stopped at the first "For-Sale" sign. Mike wrote the phone number down, but then there was another one right across the street, and then another down the block, and an entire row of them in the distance. If the "For-Sale" signs were any indication, this town seemed to be ailing. Mike recorded the phone number for each one and said he had known that many people were leaving the town; there was a tremendous amount of property for sale in Arcadia.

He directed me toward the town center. As we passed a two-story, eight-unit house, Mike commented that it had already sold for $249,000, but that it didn't matter as it was so far out of his price range. I couldn't let that pass and told him that you never know; a building of that size might work for him. He shouldn't be put off by what, to him, was a high price. It is the entire package that has to make sense. It doesn't matter what it costs, so long as the income exceeds the outgo.

His vision was slowly beginning to expand, and the fear of the numbers was beginning to subside. He and Livy didn't have a lot of money for a down payment but hearing how Wellsley and Matt had purchased a thirty-unit complex in North Carolina for no money down had obviously piqued his interest.

We toured the main street. There were a number of two-story buildings from the 1920s and 1930s. Their ground floor stores were all occupied. The street was clean and well-kept. The area was designated as an historic district, and it had a certain charm of central Florida—almost Western and ranch-like.

Mike told me that the last hurricane had bypassed the downtown, but that it had "crumpled them" out in the country. I asked him what the industry was in Arcadia. He didn't really know, but then he said it seemed to him that it was just society "living on itself"—service businesses, schools, hospitals, no real industry that he knew of, but lots of farming in the area. The population was about 6,600, and it had been fairly stable. There were a lot of migrant workers, and rentals in the area were often month to month. It's not like along the coast, where hordes of people come to retire, he told me, but even there, he said, values had tanked. He commented that some people did come to Arcadia though, because they found it to be a peaceful and settled atmosphere.

It certainly was not the active rental market adjacent to Cornell University and Ithaca College in upstate New York, but it was a pleasant town, and the obvious down market would probably present a few good opportunities for "buying a problem."

We drove on, and Mike pointed out a two-story frame house on a main street. It had blue tarps covering the roof, and two workers were up on the top beginning the reroofing process. He had been interested in it. It had seemed a manageable size to him, but it had just sold for $17,000. He said that he and Carol had looked at it when she was there a couple of weeks ago, and he had later called about it, only to find that it had been sold. Mike said that since the crash, it seemed like most people still had a very inflated idea of what their house was worth, but this one was a real fixer-upper in what he felt was his price range, and he was sorry he had missed it.

Was there really a rental market in Arcadia? With so much for sale and prices so high for a well-kept property, were people still coming to the area? And I asked how he would go about finding out what a realistic value was on a property.

Mike said that he and Livy still had people stopping by to ask them about renting their mobile home. He thought there was still interest in the area. He explained that rents ran $600 to $650 for a two-bedroom, two-bathroom house; his sense was there was still a rental market. We continued driving, passing one-story houses with for-sale signs on virtually every block. I pointed out a large two-story house to him. There was no sign on it, but it was run-down and just might be for sale. We drove up and stopped in front. It was obviously vacant, and it was run-down. The grass was overgrown, and some windows were broken. Two young boys were riding bikes in the street. Mike went over and asked them if anybody lived in the house. The older of the two boys said he didn't think so, but that someone came up on weekends. They would do a little work on it and then leave, he said.

It didn't sound too promising, we agreed. Somebody probably already had bought it and was renovating it. But I repeated to Mike that you never know until you make the effort to ask. It was entirely possible that if it had been sold, and if the new owners were doing the work on it themselves, they may have just had enough to want to sell it. We walked around back. There was a pool and a garage with holes in the roof. I suggested that Mike write down the address. He agreed with me that it was definitely worth finding out about. We got back into the car and continued our search.

Two blocks later, I pulled over to the curb and pointed out another house for Mike to take in. We were staring at a vacant two-story, wood-frame house with an upstairs porch, nice trim detail, almost Victorian with its trellis work. It was certainly large enough to be turned into a four-family house, and if the exterior's faded white paint was any indication of the rest of the house, it was just aching for a developer to take it over and renovate it. It was right across the street from a church and city hall. I pointed out to Mike that although the house was run-down and obviously in need of major repair, the church and city hall indicated that it was probably a stable area. I suggested to Mike that we should find out who the owner was to see how it was zoned.

Mike asked me how we would go about that, and I explained that we could find all the information we needed at the county assessor's office. We would be able to find the owners for both properties. We could find out how they were zoned. It would all be a matter of public record. First, we would find the tax rolls, and from that we would be able to get the name and address of the owner. Looking at my watch, it was four o'clock on Friday afternoon.

Mike said they probably closed at 4:30 p.m. so we'd better get going. He directed me back across town to an attractive, modern brick building. Mike led the way to the tax assessor's office on the first floor. At the window, he asked a young woman if she could assist us in finding the owners of two downtown properties. He gave her the addresses, and she disappeared into the back room.

I suggested that Mike go upstairs to see if he could find out the zoning for these properties while I waited. We needed to know if they were zoned single family, or if they could be converted to multifamily. Mike left to run upstairs, and in a few minutes the clerk returned with printouts for the two properties. They included the owner information, the tax information, and rates for the properties. She also gave me the website for the county assessor's office and explained that we could look up any property in the county online. We no longer needed to come into the office for this information. I thanked her, and met Mike returning down the hall. He told me we had to go across town to city hall. The county assessor didn't have details about city property. It was 4:15 p.m. We could drive back across town and just make it to the zoning office before it closed for the weekend.

I handed Mike the printouts from the tax assessor's office and suggested he call the owners while I drove. One was in Naples. He found the other by dialing *411 Connect* on his cell phone. Just as we pulled up in front of city hall, Mike called and left messages for the owners of both properties. We stood at the counter while a city employee pulled out the zoning map and spread it before us. She looked past us at the clock. I laughed and said we were sure this was just what she wanted to do five minutes before closing for the weekend, but she smiled and said it was okay. Mike and I pored over the map. We had the two addresses. We found the outline of the different zoning areas on the map. One property was "B-2," and the other "R-3." We asked the clerk if she knew what the zoning restrictions were in each area. It was 4:27. We were pushing it now, but she dutifully pulled out the four-inch-thick zoning ordinance and began thumbing through it. She found "B-2." We scanned it, and it wasn't immediately apparent whether these areas were limited to single-family houses or could be converted to multifamily. We asked her if apartments were allowed in the "B-2" zone. She didn't know but said that we could contact the zoning officer on Monday—he had already left for the day. It was exactly 4:30 p.m., so we thanked her and walked out.

Mike and I had done well. We didn't have all the answers yet, but we had found out who the owners were, we had learned what the zoning was for the properties, and we would get answers on the zoning restrictions on Monday. I mentioned to Mike that perhaps he would hear back on the weekend from the owners he had left messages with. We were on our way.

This was new territory for Mike, but he was getting into the sleuthing process, and he was realizing there were more ways to buy property than just calling the number on a Realtor's sign. I asked him if he was willing to keep looking. He was, and I asked what the best areas of town were. He said the north and west areas were the best, and he told me to turn at the next corner.

As soon as we turned, I hit the brakes. Mike saw it too. On the corner was an attractive one-story brick house with a nicely fenced-in yard and a Century 21 sign in front of it. The house appeared to be vacant, although the lawn had been recently mown.

What did Mike think? It looked good to him; we pulled over to the curb. It was ten minutes to five, but we both agreed it was worth a call to the Realtor. The Realtor was an hour away in Fort Myers. He said he was too busy to show us the property this weekend, but he could meet us on Monday. The property had recently been reduced, he said, from $103,000 to $39,900. This huge reduction sounded highly suspicious to both of us. This was obviously a distressed market.

The property was attractive from the outside. The front door was locked, so we walked around and peered in the windows. The carpet had been pulled up. The subfloor, from what we could see, was uneven and ratty. A few windows were broken. We went around back, and Mike squeezed through a small door underneath the house into the crawl space. He hollered out that basically it seemed all right. He said it looked well supported; the plumbing was intact; the wiring might need some work—it was sort of hanging down, he said, as he crawled out of the opening. He looked up at the roof, and after a brief pause, he said it looked good— almost new.

Mike looked at properties with the experienced eye of a contractor; he knew what it would take to bring them up to building code to make them habitable. I looked at them with the eye of how much money could they make. What did Mike think this house would rent for in today's market? He thought it would rent for $650 a month. He felt that the market had really come down in the past year, but that for a single-family house in good condition, $650 was probably a safe number. We decided to figure it out and pulling out my pocket calculator, we walked over and sat on the edge of the brick front porch.

Was $650 really the highest rent for a single house? In Ithaca, a similar house would rent for twice that amount. Mike said that in this market he'd be nervous trying to get any more than that. We discussed who would pay the utilities—the tenant or the owner? He said typically the owner would pay utilities. And the taxes? Same answer—the owner. How much would the taxes be? Mike thought for a moment and said that he and Livy paid around $400 per month for taxes and insurance. How much was his property was assessed for? He told me $197,000. Calculating the ratio of $39,900 to $197,000 we came up with $67 per month for taxes on this house. This was really a rough guess at this point, but it was a working number. Based on what he paid at home, he thought insurance would be another $35 per month, so based on Mike's estimate, taxes and insurance would cost around $105 per month. He thought $50 per month for maintenance should be okay. I suggested he add another 6.5% of the total rent for management, or $45 per month. We charged 6.5% at home to manage our own properties. But in this case it would be money in Mike's pocket, because he and Livy would likely do all the advertising, renting, bookkeeping, and the taking of tenant calls—between them they could do a complete job of the management. He agreed.

We punched in the numbers on the calculator—$105 for taxes and insurance, $45 for management, $50 for maintenance and upkeep. The total was $200 for expenses on the one-bedroom house. That left $450 from the income available for debt service to the bank and return to the owner. There are always unexpected expenses owning properties. Mike would make some money from the management fee, but he would have to pay for ads and his phone. Although he could do most of the maintenance himself he would have to pay for gas for the lawnmower, and paint, and probably a broken window now and then.

Eventually he would have major expenses such as the roof and a water heater, and it would probably be best to save some of his maintenance costs in a reserve for future expenses and not count on it all as spendable income.

The cost of financing $39,900 was the next calculation we had to make. Punching the number into my real estate calculator—$39,900 present value. For an interest rate, we would assume 7% (based on what local banks in Ithaca were offering at that time, finding a rate in the 6% range was no longer a possibility). We entered 7% interest. For the term, usually the banks would let you finance a loan over twenty to thirty years. We assumed for the moment a loan for twenty-five years at 7%.

We used the full amount of $39,900 because even if he had to come up with 20-25% equity (down payment) he would want a return on that. And besides, we were hoping to find a way for the seller to finance the difference between

what the bank would lend and what Mike would finally negotiate for the purchase price. The cost to amortize the full
amount of the loan of $39,900, for 25 years at 7% interest,
would be $282 per month for principal and interest. Princi-
pal, I explained to Mike, was the amount of the original loan
he would be paying back each month. Interest was the cost
of borrowing the remaining amount due on the loan each
month. Subtract $282 from the $450, and at least on our first
pass, Mike could make $168 per month, provided the house
was in move-in condition. However, looking in the windows,
we could tell that it was far from move-in condition.

Additionally, we needed to find out what it would cost
to make the house habitable. From what he had seen looking through the windows, what did he think would have to
spend to bring the property up to rentable condition? Without being able to get inside, it was all a guess at this point,
but Mike took a stab at it. It would certainly need flooring. It
would probably need air conditioning.

He thought the exterior was in good shape. The brick
was attractive, and the mortar appeared to be sound. The
roof looked fairly new. Mike thought the windows should
be replaced with energy-efficient windows. He said the state
of Florida offered a rebate on the cost of energy-efficient
windows. What did he think the windows would cost? He
said probably $225 to $250 per window but he would check
it online when we got home to get the exact number. We
counted fourteen windows. At $225 per window, they would
cost $3,150.

How much would he allow for flooring? He said he had
put down laminate at home. It has a wood look and it had

cost $1.80 per square foot. Mike said that the Realtor had told him the house listed at 2,100 square feet. We multiplied it out—$3,780. Mike thought that was about right for the material. If he did the installation, it shouldn't cost any more than that.

Mike guessed that the air conditioning would cost about $4,500. He looked around and pointed out that the trim needed to be painted and the yard needed a good cleanup. He thought that if he did it all, it would cost about $500 for paint and shrubs. He and Livy could plant the shrubs, and he had a paint sprayer. For miscellaneous cleanup inside and renting a dumpster to haul off the trash, he estimated another $500. This was good, and we added up what was a back-of-the-envelope analysis of what it should cost to bring the house up to the level of finish for Mike to rent it: windows $3,150; flooring $3,780; AC $4,500; painting, shrubs, and miscellaneous $1,000. It totaled $12,430. We agreed on $12,500 as a safe number based on what we had seen looking through the windows, underneath in the crawl space, and just walking around the property.

If he was no longer working for his general contractor, he would have to replace his income somehow. He said his wage was typically $15 an hour. That was adequate. We multiplied 160 hours times $15 per hour—Mike's labor would add another $2,400 to the job. Totaling the cost of materials and Mike's labor, we had a total of $14,900 which we rounded up to $15,000. Mike thought that was reasonable. I cautioned him that this was all preliminary and that he shouldn't get attached to any of it. What we were trying to do in a first pass was to back into a purchase price. If he and Livy could buy this house for the asking price and spend an additional $15,000 on restoring it to good condition, would it be worth it? Was the market actually there for renting it? If they couldn't buy it and renovate it for the number they needed, or if, after looking at the Arcadia rental market, he didn't think it would rent, then it would be best not to pursue it.

Mike's goal had been to make $150 a month from his first property. The seller was asking $39,900. If Mike chose to do the work himself, he could pay himself $15 per hour during the renovation, or he could afford to hire someone to work for that amount and do the work for him. Considering the cost of the renovation, how much could he then afford to pay for the property? We knew that he had $450 per month net operating income, after taking into account all expenses: $650 in rent minus $200 in expenses. We knew it would cost approximately $15,000 to renovate the property. We then assumed that he would have to finance not only the purchase price but also the renovation cost. We calculated that $15,000 for the renovation at 7%, over a twenty-five-year term, would cost an additional $106 per month. That, plus the $150 Mike wanted to make as a return to himself in order to make it worthwhile to take the risk of renovating the property and renting it for the next twenty-five years, totaled $256. Subtracting $256 from the $450, he had in net operating income left $194 he could afford in debt service above the $15,000 he needed for renovation.

How much could Mike afford to pay for the house if this were the case? If he had to have $194 per month available for additional debt service, how much could he then afford to pay and still make his $150 per month? Entering the payment of $194 at 7% interest, twenty-five-year term into my real estate calculator—the answer was $27,448. Rounding it off, we agreed he could pay $27,500. Mike asked me if it was reasonable to think the seller would come down that far. My response was that you never know until you ask. This was a down market. The seller had already reduced the price significantly. It was worth asking.

I suggested that Mike call the Realtor back to see if someone else could show us the property. It didn't hurt to push limits a little bit—his own and the Realtor's. After all, he was trying to buy a house, and it was the Realtor's job to show it to him. He should push back a little bit. Mike made the call and the Realtor agreed to have one of his associates call Mike that evening.

On the way home, we drove back by the two houses we had seen earlier. We agreed they were both beauties. If zoning allowed for them to be divided up into four units each, they might be a possibility. At home, Mike showed me his loan book—an amortization book where he could look up the same numbers we had been able to figure in my real estate calculator. He also had a real estate calculator, with which he could do the calculations to find the cost per month of a loan at any specified interest rate and term of amortization, or repayment. These were basic tools he would need as he looked further at properties. He found them simple to use.

After having dinner and spending some time with Livy, Carol and the baby, Mike and I went into his office and looked up 519 N. Arcadia on the internet. On the website for the county assessor's office, we could find out exactly how much the taxes were on the property. Mike pulled it up in no time. He had already studied and learned to decipher the printouts from the two properties we had received at the assessor's office, so this one was easy. The property was assessed at $46,400, so the taxes were based on that price. The total cost of the taxes was listed for 2008 at $1,640. That skewed our numbers. We had estimated that taxes would cost $67 per month or $804 per year. We changed the tax amount to $137 per month, which was the $1,640 total annual taxes divided by 12 months. That lowered the amount of return to Mike by $70 a month. Instead of making $150 a month on the property, he would make $80. It began to look less attractive. I suggested we lower the price and see what the effect would be. Mike looked up an $80 per month payment in his amortization book—an even $11,000 would cost him $77.75 a month. It made sense that for Mike to make his goal of $150 per month he needed to negotiate another $11,000 off the purchase price. Since the taxes would cost him another $80 per month, he could not pay the $27,500 we had initially calculated he could pay, after taking the renovation cost into account. Now he could pay $16,500.

Mike looked up and shook his head. The seller would never come down that far. They would never take a price that much lower than the asking price. The original asking price had been $103,000; this was obviously a fire sale. Someone really wanted to get rid of this place. He should not get attached to the house, nor to his assumption as to what the seller would do. If he wanted to make $150 a month on this particular deal, the numbers dictated what he could pay. It was basically a nice property, at least from the outside. He should just wait and see what they say once we are able to hook up with the Realtor. He would never know until he asked. Mike's cell phone rang, and the Realtor agreed to meet us at 2:30 on Saturday at the property. Pushing back a little had worked.

Mike's friend from Port Charlotte called right after that. He had made a mistake about what his father had for sale. It was not four four-unit properties, but rather four two-unit properties at $179,000 for each building. Sixteen units had evaporated down to eight. Four buildings at $179,000 each totaled $716,000. Sixteen units would have cost $44,750 per unit. Now the $716,000 covered only eight units, which would mean that Mike would have to pay $89,500 per unit.

Would that work for Mike? He began calculating. His friend had told him that the units rented for $650 for each side of the duplex for a total of $1,300 per month income from each building. Mike opened up his amortization book and looked up an even $180,000 at 7% interest, twenty-five-year term. The debt service alone would cost $1,272.20 per month. That left nothing for taxes, insurance, and upkeep, much less money for Mike and Livy. As a four-plex at that price, it would have made sense. As a duplex, it was completely overpriced based on the income. Mike had done his calculations. He was getting the picture.

We sat for a while and went back over our day together—calling Realtors, going to the assessor's office, going to the zoning office, finding two properties that weren't even listed but that looked interesting, and researching the owners and tax assessments at the county offices. What had Mike learned? He began listing what he had taken away from the day. He had found there was an awful lot out there for sale, with a wide range of purchase prices. He learned that he had gained enough confidence that he could probably do the financial analysis of how to buy a property. He had learned how to research the details of a property in the assessor's office or online. He had learned how to look up the zoning. Mike said that he felt he could buy a property. It didn't seem that difficult to him. He said he wasn't totally sure he had the confidence he needed to do it yet, but it was starting to make sense.

I asked Mike now much money he and Livy had. He said they had refinanced the house and pulled out about $15,000 to use while Livy was having the baby. They still had most of that. He said they also had $130,000 available on credit cards, not that they would ever use it, but they had been approved for that from various banks. He said they had excellent credit. That would be useful, but it would be best not to use credit cards for purchasing a house since the interest rates were well over 20%. It was nice to know that funds were available in an emergency. I asked Mike if they could use, say $5,000 of their available cash, as a down payment, if it were to be required. He said they could do that.

The next morning Mike and I walked around the pond feeding the goats, the geese, and Toby the pony. In the back pasture Mike pointed out a tortoise lying quietly in the grass right at the fence line. On the other side of the fence he pointed out the five-acre fenced-in parcel. He and Livy had thought for several years they should buy it and build a rental property there.

We finished feeding the animals and went back into the house. I suggested we sit down and analyze the five-acre parcel and their idea of building a rental property on it. It would be good to check out whatever options they had for improving their income. Livy joined us with the baby. How much did the neighbors want for the land? Livy said they were asking $100,000. Did they know the zoning? Livy said they could have one dwelling unit on the five acres.

It was a little surprising they couldn't build at least a four-plex or even just a duplex on five acres, but she reaffirmed that the zoning would allow only a single unit. She added that it could be up to four or even five bedrooms, but there could be only one dwelling unit. I asked how much rent they would be able to charge on a single unit.

Livy had been the one responsible for renting their mobile unit next door, so she had an idea of the market. She said they could probably get between $650 and $800. A year ago, they could have gotten $1,000 to $1,200, but rents had dropped considerably in the past year. I asked Mike what it would cost to build a three-bedroom house—how much a square foot would he charge? He thought he could build a 2,000-square-foot house, which would equate with four or five bedrooms, for $125 a square foot.

We began calculating. It would cost $250,000 to build the house. Mike agreed that sounded about right. The land would cost another $100,000. If they were able to finance the entire project of $350,000 at 7% interest over a twenty-five-year amortization, what would it cost?

Mike pulled out his real estate amortization book; $350,000 at 7% for twenty-five years would cost $2,473.73 per month in debt service alone. He was beginning to see that if they received $650 in rent, it would cost them $1,823.72

a month to buy the property, build the house, and rent it out for $650 a month. By the time they had added taxes and insurance, they would be in the hole another $400 to $500. They realized that it would cost them $2,200 to $2,400 a month in negative cash flow to build a house for rental on the land next door, and obviously it was not a deal they would want to pursue.

This had been a pipe dream of theirs for several years, and we had just shattered it by running the numbers. They understood that if zoning allowed them to put up six or eight units next door, and if they could rent the units for $650 each, for a 1,000 to 1,200-square-foot unit, they might have a chance. But the zoning here was too restrictive. The numbers didn't lie. Livy and Mike could not make money building a new house next door. They agreed that it was a fantasy they would have to give up, and that it was not worth their time to consider it further. Running the numbers had given them a strong dose of reality.

At its most basic, real estate is a numbers game. In my opinion, the best way to get started toward creating an independent income in real estate was to find a property that needed renovation, one that had been let go, one that they could purchase for a fraction of what it would cost to build new. Mike could do the renovation, and later on, after they had gained experience and built an equity base, they could think about new construction.

I suggested to Mike that we analyze the property we looked at yesterday. We knew that it had a floor area of approximately 2,100 square feet. What it would cost to build this house new? Mike thought for a moment and said again that he could build a house new for about $125/sq. ft. We multiplied it out and figured that a newly constructed house on that site would cost $262,500 to build. If Mike and Livy paid the bank's new asking price of $39,900 on the 519 N. Arcadia property, the cost per square foot including the lot, the city sewer, and water hook-ups would be $19. The house suddenly seemed like a good deal to them, but it wasn't. They still had to take into account the $15,000 of renovation to make it habitable. If they paid $39,900, and still wanted to make their $150 per month clear, they would have paid too much. We calculated it as follows:

$39,900 plus $15,000 is $54,900. Mike looked up the cost of that in his amortization book. The principal and interest payment on a loan of $54,900 would cost them $388 per month. If the property made $450 per month net operating income, as we had calculated earlier, they would be left with $62 per month. They would have to decide if it was worth all the effort to renovate that house and make $62 per month.

However, if they could buy it at the number we had calculated it was worth ($16,500), and if Mike could do the renovations for the $15,000 he had estimated, the total price would equate to around $31,500 or $15 per square foot, and they would make their goal of $150 per month. It was worth no more than that based on what the rental market would produce for them in income, and certainly, in the market they were in, which would allow only $650 per month in rent for a three-bedroom house, they would be a little short of crazy to build a new rental house for $262,500. They agreed with that.

What they were buying when they bought a rental property was an income stream—possibly some appreciation or increase in value over time, but primarily they were buying an income stream, and they would want to make sure in their initial analysis that their income exceeded their outgo. In addition, it was important that they have a positive cash flow in their initial calculations, because there would always be something unexpected. And they could see from our cost comparison of a newly built home that it would be much safer to buy a rental property already built than to build new.

That afternoon at 2:30 p.m., Mike and I met Ralph, the Realtor, at the property at 519 N. Arcadia. He had driven up from Port Charlotte. Ralph knew little about the property except that it was in foreclosure, which he said explained the dramatic price drop. It had started out at $103,000 a month ago. It had dropped to $89,000, then $83,000. A week ago, the bank was asking $46,900, and just this week it dropped again to $39,900. When we went inside, we could see why. While the exterior was an attractive, uniform brick façade, the interior had ceilings at varying levels room to room, some not as high as seven feet. The entire floor was unsteady and covered with particle board. Rats had chewed several large holes along the edges of the rooms. The floor bounced. Another large hole had been poked through one of the bedroom floors, exposing the termite-infested floor joists. Here was a real fixer-upper.

We had pushed to get into the property over the weekend. It had looked good from the outside. Now Mike was somewhat staggered by the magnitude of the job to be done. It was twice the work he had thought, or even more.

Ralph began selling us. He had been a contractor back in Kentucky, and he thought the best way to approach this house would be to tear up the entire floor system. Clean it out. Reinstall floor joists and subflooring and go from there. It seemed reasonable. While the floor system was open, you would have access to the crawl space from above and be able to do any rewiring or re-plumbing. Getting rid of the particle-board flooring would probably get rid of most of the moisture and mold that permeated the house. We asked Ralph if he could leave the keys to the house so we could spend some time going through it. He couldn't do that, but what we did after he left, he said, was our business. We had seen that the door at the rear of the house had a broken window and reaching in to unlock the lock would not be difficult. Ralph turned to go and then paused. He told us that he was not trying to influence us one way or the other, but that it was a good price for the house in spite of the work. He suggested that we make the bank an offer. It would have to go through Wachovia's foreclosure section in Tampa, but he would submit an offer directly to them.

Mike told him his impression of the property—that from looking in through the windows yesterday, he had thought it might take $15,000 to renovate it. From going through it, he could see that it was going to take two, if not three, times that to bring it back to habitable condition. He asked Ralph if he thought the bank would entertain an offer for ten, or even seven thousand dollars.

Ralph was quick to respond. He said he doubted they would go that low, that they had already reduced the asking price from $103,000. But then he suggested that Mike figure out what he thought it would cost to renovate and then give Ralph his best offer, and he would submit it. He would be available Monday, and Mike could send it to him. Mike thanked him for making the trip all the way from Port Charlotte. This deal would obviously not be much of a money maker in commission for Ralph, but he was a professional and took it in stride. He left us sitting on the front stoop again with our calculator and a notepad.

Mike was still reeling from the magnitude of the project. He didn't know where to start; he suggested we go back inside. I said that we could probably sit right where we were and come up with a pretty good estimate of what it would cost to rehab the house. It was certainly a derelict, but it was worth at least going through the analysis.

Mike should put on his contractor's hat. How would he approach this if he were looking at it for a customer?

That was easy for him. He liked Ralph's idea of tearing up and replacing the floor. He jumped up and said he would be right back. He was going to pace off the footprint. He walked down the long side of the building and yelled back that it was one hundred eighty feet long. It couldn't be. I had looked at enough buildings, and this one wasn't half as long as a football field. Mike walked it again with his long (three-foot) stride and agreed with me. He had been counting by threes. The building was sixty feet long. He paced off the width at the front side of the building—thirty-five feet. It was exactly the 2,100 square feet they were billing it as.

I asked Mike to take me through the entire process. How would he begin this job if it were for a client? He barely paused. He'd do the demolition first. He would tear out all the termite-infested joists and the subflooring. He'd have an exterminator come in and "tent" the house. That was new terminology for me. He explained that in Florida, they put a tent over the entire house, spray in Zoecon, an insecticide, let it sit, and within a day or two, you have a clean house. By doing the demo first, he would open up most of the infested areas so that he would get a better job of extermination. The cost? Probably around $2,000 for a house of this size was his estimate. After that, while the floor was out and the crawl space exposed, he'd go in and redo any plumbing and wiring required. We had thought about moving the kitchen, and he agreed that would be next. This would allow him to create a fourth bedroom, making the house more competitive in the rental market. He'd plumb for the kitchen while the crawl space was exposed.

How much it would cost to do the floor? He began the calculation while I wrote down his estimates: Using pressure-treated 2" x 8" floor joists on 16 inch centers for 60 feet he'd need 45 spans, and going three across, he'd need 3 pieces for each span—that's 135. Plus he'd need more for the perimeter plate to hang the joists from—say another 16. We agreed on 150, but to be safe we rounded it up to 170. How much would they cost apiece? His estimate was $12 each. Multiplying it out, we had a number of $2,040 for the joists and perimeter board. How much subflooring and what would he use? Mike would use ¾ inch plywood. It was heavy-duty and didn't have to be pressure treated. 2,100 square feet divided by 32 square feet (a 4' x 8' piece of plywood) yielded 66 sheets. Again we agreed on a cushion and rounded up to 70 sheets. Mike's cost estimate—$35 per sheet. Calculating it out—$2,450. Mike said that sounded reasonable. The entire list of materials for the floor system would cost $4,490. We rounded it up to $5,000. How long it would take him to install the new system? He figured four full days working alone ought to do it—32 hours at Mike's salary of $15 per hour was $480.

Framing in the new hall, adding new sheet rock, moving the kitchen, and painting—Mike estimated $3,000 for that and added another $500 for millwork, trim and so on. We'd already estimated windows and painting. We totaled it out and agreed we had a pretty good idea of the cost to restore the house to rentable condition, and we didn't even have to do a breaking and entering job to get it. I suggested we drive over and look at the new subsidized units—his competition.

We got into Mike's truck and headed across town. Mike didn't know the entire story, but he thought the City of Arcadia had collaborated with a private developer to construct 250 units of subsidized housing at the edge of town. Wal-Mart had built a distribution super center several miles out of town, and they obviously needed housing for their employees; 250 new units on the market in this town would help explain the huge rise in vacancies locally and the many houses for sale. We arrived at the new aluminum-sided two-story complex. They were obviously low budget, but they were attractive and brand new, and based on the sparse number of cars there late on a Saturday afternoon, they were not yet fully rented. This project was going to present some serious competition in the Arcadia rental market. It would be good to find out what the units rented for, and how many they still had to rent. Mike said he would do that on Monday. We drove toward home. On reaching the intersection with the main road, I asked Mike to turn right because I had a hunch there might be something that way. He turned onto Route 70 East, also known on the highway sign as East Magnolia. And there it was—ahead of us on the right was a magnificent three-story Spanish-style home. It was obviously vacant. It was on the main road, and there was no place to park, so Mike turned at the first cross street, and we drove around the block. Before we came back to the main road, on our right, adjacent to the lovely three-story home, was another three-story building built in the same Spanish-style architecture. The windows had been broken, and the white paint was peeling off the brick. We drove in and around the back. Mike pointed out there were seven electrical meters— six units and a house meter. We got out of the car and walked to the back of the building. The rear doors were locked, but it was evident that here was a building configured as apartments, vacant and run-down, but nonetheless, a building with huge potential.

We bushwhacked across the yard and through the underbrush to the original building along the main road. On the way we stumbled on a concrete rim protruding from the weeds—probably a once beautiful goldfish pond, now filled with dirt. Mike and I smiled at each other. This had surely been a magnificent place in its day. We arrived at the Century 21 sign in the front yard of this magnificent derelict mansion. Why hadn't the Realtor mentioned this one to us? Mike pointed out that it was a different phone number. The Century 21 Realtor on the 519 N. Arcadia property was a Port Charlotte number. This one was a local number. Mike should call it. We walked up the wide stairs onto the front porch and peered in through the glass of the huge double doors. He dialed the local number and ended up leaving a message for them to call him back.

Inside, we could see the structure had been totally gutted. There was a magnificent staircase still intact leading to the second floor. We could see light reflecting down the stairs from a large opening in the roof. Someone had great plans for this building and had abandoned it partway through a renovation. This building was a real opportunity if it could be bought at the right price.

That evening, Mike and I sat and worked up a series of Excel spreadsheets for the purchase, renovation, and operation of 519 N. Arcadia. The East Magnolia Street property was intriguing, but 519 was the most real of his options for now. Here's how things looked so far:

CONSTRUCTION BUDGET - 519 N. ARCADIA AVE. ARCADIA, FLORIDA MIKE & LIVY

Item	Unit Cost	Task	Materials	Hours	Labor
Building Permit		PERMITS & FEES	$500		
Subfloor Removal		DEMOLITION	$0	36	$540
2 - 40 yd. Dumpsters	$1,000	TRASH REMOVAL	$2,000		
Tent entire house		EXTERMINATING	$2,000		
60' x 36', 16" on center + Per. 2" x 8" x 12"—170 pcs.	$10.97	FLOOR JOISTS	$1,870	32	$480
Relocate Kitchen		PLUMBING UPGRADE	$2,000		
		ELECTRICAL UPGRADE	$2,000		
Install 4' x 8' x 3/4" plywood $35 x 70 sheets	$35.00	SUBFLOOR	$2,450	32	$480
		HALLWAY/SF/FRAMING	$3,000	50	$750
		RELOCATE KITCHEN	$2,000	32	$480

Item	Unit Cost	Task	Materials	Hours	Labor
14 windows	$200.00	WINDOWS	$2,800	50	$750
		PAINT	$500	32	$480
		MILLWORK	$500	32	$480
Laminate throughout		FLOORING	$4,500	48	$720
	$200.00	REPLACE FRONT DOOR	$200	6	$90
		LANDSCAPING	$200	30	$450
		HVAC	$4,300		
		TOTAL	**$30,820**	**380**	**$5,700**
3%		GENERAL CONDITIONS	$925		
8%		CONTINGENCY	$2,540		
Labor, Materials, GC, Contingency		**PROJECT COST**	**$39,984**		

Mike had researched the actual costs of the 2" x 8" floor joists online. He also had a better cost on the windows. He had decided rather than just patch and paint the front door it would be better to install a new one. We "guesstimated" $4,300 for the AC. This would have to be confirmed with an HVAC contractor, if he and Livy decided to proceed. But it seemed like a good enough number for now. He could tile the bathrooms and replace the fixtures, he thought, for $2,000. Otherwise, the numbers were about where we had estimated the day before, except for the extensive work that had to be done on the flooring. At my suggestion, Mike added some money for general conditions and an 8% contingency. He had a $40,000 renovation on his hands.

I asked Mike if this was how he usually went about estimating his projects. He said it was the same idea, except the architect for a building would do the initial estimate. Once that looked reasonable, he said the contractor worked it through with his material take-offs and labor costs. But yes, they followed this basic process, only on a larger scale.

Next let's look at how this would affect the purchase price for the project, in fact, let's build a purchase analysis sheet for starters. This is what we did:

PROPERTY - 519 N. Arcadia Ave.	ASKING PRICE: $39,900	Debt Service	Mortgage	Interest	Term
	Offering Price **$16,500**	($343.25)	$50,836	6.50%	300
4 Bedroom, 2 bath	Rehab Amount $39,984				
90%	Total Loan Amount (90%) $50,836				
Assume 10%	Equity Required $5,648				
	Total Project Cost **$56,484**				
	Gross Income/Month **$695**				
	EXPENSES/MONTH				
	Taxes $137				
	Insurance $35				
	Management $25				
	Maintenance $50				
	TOTAL EXPENSES **$247**				

PROPERTY - 519 N. Arcadia Ave. (continued)	ASKING PRICE:	$39,900	Debt Service	Mortgage	Interest	Term
A bit subjective, but your banker will tell what they use in the area	Cap Rate	8.00%				
Divide NOI by cap rate	Value upon renovation	$67,250				
The Excel formula is =pymt(int.rate/12, # of pymts, mtg. amount) Excel will calculate the debt service per month.	Debt Service	$343				
Divide the cash flow by the debt service. Banks usually require at least 1.2 debt service coverage	Debt Service Coverage	1.3				
Less than desired but still worthwhile.	Cash Flow	$105				
(Keep this to yourself)	% Return on Equity	22%				

Mike realized that he could transfer these formats to an Excel spreadsheet, and by using the formulas indicated, he would have a useful tool for analyzing any renovation project and then backing into a purchase price. He would have to negotiate the deal, of course, but he now had at least a rational basis on which to make an offer on any property and keep out of trouble. I told him to leave off the return on equity when he showed his analysis to a bank. Ideally he would like to have an infinite return by putting in $0 and reaping whatever cash flow the property will generate, but typically in my experience, bankers don't get very enthusiastic about that approach. On the 519 N. Arcadia property, the Realtor had told us he thought the bank would at least look at a purchase offer with only 10% down, and he and Livy had that available from the refinance of their house if they needed it.

Mike calculated that upon completion of the renovation, the value of the property would be $67,250. The project cost was approximately $56,484. Once the renovation was complete and the property was rented, Mike and Livy would have immediately created additional equity in the project of over $10,700.

Next we developed an operating budget. I shared with him the basic format used on a property whether it is just a few units or a property worth millions.

PREPARED FOR: 519 N. Arcadia St., Arcadia, FL	PREPARED BY: Mike & Livy Arcadia, FL	
ASSUMPTIONS	**INCOME**	**MONTHLY BUDGET**
	Gross Potential Rent	$695
5.00%	Vacancy	$(35)
	Effective Rent	$660
	TOTAL INCOME	**$660**
	EXPENSES	
	MAINTENANCE	
	Exterminating	
	Landscape	
	Lawn Mowing	
Mike does the work	Materials/Supplies	$50
	Maintenance Labor	
	TOTAL MAINTENANCE	**$50**
Livy handles mgmt.	**MANAGEMENT**	
	Advertising	
	Tenant Relations	
	Legal	
	Accouting	
	Write Off	
	Collection Exp.	
6.50%	Management Fee	$25
	Total Management	**$25**
Estimate—need firm quote	**INSURANCE**	
	Property Insurance	$35
	Umbrella	
	Liability Insurance	
	Total Insurance	**$35**
Paid by Tenant	**UTILITIES**	
	Water & Sewer	
	Electricity	
	Gas Utility	
	Trash Removal	
	Solid Waste Fee	
	Total Utilities	
Need actual breakdown	**TAXES**	
	City Taxes	$137
	School Taxes	
	County Taxes	
	Total Taxes	**$137**

ASSUMPTIONS	INCOME	MONTHLY BUDGET
	TOTAL OPERATING EXPENSES	$247
	NET OPERATING INCOME	$414
	OTHER TRANSACTIONS	
Enter from amortization schedule	Principal & Interest on 1st Mortgage	$343
	Principal 1st Mortgage	
	Capital Imp. Incl. Carpet	
	Appliances	
	Furniture & Equipment	
	Total Other Transactions	$343
89.35%	TOTAL EXPENSES	$590
	CASH FLOW	**$70**

This was a far cry from the original $150 a month in cash flow that had been our bottom line. We talked it over. If Mike and Livy were to offer $16,500 for the property and take into account the nearly $40,000 needed for the renovation, and if they took into account the minimum of 10% down that the bank would require, if they chose to do the deal, this is the best they could do. We even assumed a lower interest rate—6.5% instead of 7%. As Mike said, his offer of $7,000 for the property would be more realistic from their point of view.

Next, we went to work on the construction schedule. Mike gave me the sequencing and time he thought it would take him to do the work for each phase of the job, and together we came up with the following scheduling chart:

FIRST & SECOND WEEK	WEEK:		1					2				
ASSUMPTION	TASK	Hours	M	T	W	T	F	M	T	W	T	F
Building Department	PERMITS & FEES		x									
2 Men, 2 days	DEMOLITION	32	x	x								
2 Men, 2 days	FLOOR JOISTS	32			x	x						
Weekly total cleanup	TRASH REMOVAL						x					x
Outside Contractor - Tent Building	EXTERMINATING						x	x	x			
	PLUMBING UPGRADE								x			
	ELECTRICAL UPGRADE								x			
2 Men, 2 days	SUBFLOOR	32								x		
2 Men, 3 days	HALLWAY/SF/FRAMING	40									x	
General Contractor (Mike)	PAINT	8										
2 Men, 2 days	RELOCATE KITCHEN	32										
GC	WINDOWS	40										
GC	MILLWORK	32										
GC	BATHROOMS FIXTURES/TILE	80										
GC	FLOORING	48										
GC	REPLACE FRONT DOOR	4										
GC	LANDSCAPING											
Outside Contractor	HVAC											
	TOTAL	380										

THIRD & FOURTH WEEK	WEEK:			3					4				
ASSUMPTION	TASK	Hours	M	T	W	T	F	M	T	W	T	F
	PERMITS & FEES											
2 Men, 2 days	DEMOLITION	32										
	TRASH REMOVAL											x
Outside Contractor - Tent Building	EXTERMINATING						x					
2 Men, 2 days	FLOOR JOISTS	32										
	PLUMBING UPGRADE											
	ELECTRICAL UPGRADE											
2 Men, 2 days	SUBFLOOR	32										
2 Men, 3 days	HALLWAY/SF/FRAMING	40	x	x	x							
GC	PAINT	8				x						
2 Men, 2 days	RELOCATE KITCHEN	32					x	x				
GC	WINDOWS	40						x	x	x	x	x
GC	MILLWORK	32										
GC	BATHROOMS FIXTURES/TILE	80										
GC	FLOORING	48										
GC	REPLACE FRONT DOOR	4										
GC	LANDSCAPING											
Outside Contractor	HVAC											
	TOTAL	380										

FIFTH & SIXTH WEEK	WEEK:			5					6				
ASSUMPTION	TASK	Hours	M	T	W	T	F	M	T	W	T	F
	PERMITS & FEES											
2 Men, 2 days	DEMOLITION	32										
Outside Contractor—Tent Building	TRASH REMOVAL						x					x
	EXTERMINATING											
2 Men, 2 days	FLOOR JOISTS	32										
	PLUMBING UPGRADE											
	ELECTRICAL UPGRADE											
2 Men, 2 days	SUBFLOOR	32										
2 Men, 3 days	HALLWAY/SF/FRAMING	40										
GC	PAINT	8										
2 Men, 2 days	RELOCATE KITCHEN	32										
GC	WINDOWS	40										
GC	MILLWORK	32	x	x	x	x						
	BATHROOMS											
GC	FIXTURES/TILE	80				x	x	x	x	x		
GC	FLOORING	48										
GC	REPLACE FRONT DOOR	4										
GC	LANDSCAPING											
Outside Contractor	HVAC											
	TOTAL	380										

SEVENTH & EIGHTH WEEK	WEEK:		7					8				
ASSUMPTION	TASK	Hours	M	T	W	T	F	M	T	W	T	F
	PERMITS & FEES											
2 Men, 2 days	DEMOLITION	32										
	TRASH REMOVAL											x
Outside Contractor - Tent Building	EXTERMINATING						x					
2 Men, 2 days	FLOOR JOISTS	32										
	PLUMBING UPGRADE											
	ELECTRICAL UPGRADE											
2 Men, 2 days	SUBFLOOR	32										
2 Men, 3 days	HALLWAY/SF/FRAMING	40										
GC	PAINT	8										
2 Men, 2 days	RELOCATE KITCHEN	32										
GC	WINDOWS	40										
GC	MILLWORK	32										
GC	BATHROOMS											
	FIXTURES/TILE	80	x	x	x							
GC	FLOORING	48				x	x	x	x	x	x	
GC	REPLACE FRONT DOOR	4										
GC	LANDSCAPING											
Outside Contractor	HVAC											x
	TOTAL	380										

NINTH WEEK	WEEK:				9		
ASSUMPTION	TASK	Hours	M	T	W	T	F
	PERMITS & FEES						
2 Men, 2 days	DEMOLITION	32					
	TRASH REMOVAL						x
Outside Contractor - Tent Building	EXTERMINATING						
2 Men, 2 days	FLOOR JOISTS	32					
	PLUMBING UPGRADE						
	ELECTRICAL UPGRADE						
2 Men, 2 days	SUBFLOOR	32					
2 Men, 3 days	HALLWAY/SF/FRAMING	40					
GC	PAINT	8					
2 Men, 2 days	RELOCATE KITCHEN	32					
GC	WINDOWS	40					
GC	MILLWORK	32					
GC	BATHROOMS FIXTURES/TILE	80					
GC	FLOORING	48					
GC	REPLACE FRONT DOOR	4					
GC	LANDSCAPING		x	x	x	x	x
Outside Contractor	HVAC		x	x	x	x	x
	TOTAL HOURS	380					

We calculated that the project would take nine weeks to complete. Mike could pay himself $15 an hour during that time, and at the end of the project, assuming it was rented, and assuming they could operate the property to the budget, they would make $70 a month. It was not a lot, but they had some money they could put down, and if the bank went along with the project, they could make it work. If they were able to renovate it and rent it, not only would Mike have been paid during construction, and not only would they have additional income of $70 per month, but they also would have created an additional $10,700 of equity. The numbers looked reasonable, but the risk they faced was whether they would even be able to rent it, much less sell it, in such a depressed market.

We had done a lot of work figuring out the construction budget, the operating budget, and the construction schedule. The Excel charts appeared detailed and a bit complex. I told Mike not to worry if the charts seemed complicated. He did not have to use them. He could do the entire process by hand on a legal pad if he was more comfortable with that. The main thing was to figure out how much rent a property would take in and then figure out all the expenses. The rent must exceed the expenses, or it would not be worth considering.

Monday, I awoke with an awesome head cold and dressed to accompany Mike for the day, but quickly realized I wasn't going anywhere. Besides, it would be good for him to be on his own now—visiting the city building department, the banks, and the Realtor for the East Magnolia Street properties. He would be on his own, after all, when Carol and I left the next day. He had the financial tools from our weekend sessions, and he had the confidence now to do this work on his own. I undressed and went back to bed.

Midday he returned home and downloaded his day's experiences so far. The Realtor for the East Magnolia Street houses said the owner was flying in today, and he would call Mike back once he had met with him. The properties were indeed for sale for around $500,000. Mike and I both agreed that was probably last year's price, before the 2008 credit debacle. He had visited the city project coordinator, who said that the City of Arcadia was pretty lax about building renovations. Most people didn't even bother to file a building permit for renovations—that explained why so many of the buildings in this town were ramshackle and unkempt. It also explained why the floors and ceilings at 519 N. Arcadia St. were so rough and uneven. Previous owners had probably just added on to the house without regard for the building code and without oversight from a building inspector.

Mike's last stop for the morning had been with Bank of America, to speak with the loan officer about what kind of financing would be available for the 519 project. The banker had told him that a year ago the bank would have financed him at 90% of the purchase price. Today, he told Mike that he would need 25% equity, and that he wouldn't do the deal anyway, because in today's market in Arcadia it was too speculative.

Mike said the banker had been very standoffish at first. Mike was good at talking with people and had begun chatting the guy up. Gradually the banker had warmed and told Mike that he had grown up in Arcadia and had a good friend who owned and rented twenty houses in the town. Two years ago, his friend had a waiting list with a dozen names on it. In the past year, tenants in eight of the houses had vacated, and the houses now sat empty. People were fleeing the town. Young people were moving back home with their parents, taking their spouses and children with them. Times were tough. And not just in Arcadia, he had told Mike, but all over the state of Florida.

We sat at the kitchen table. Mike picked through his lunch. He was depressed. His conversation with the banker had taken the wind out of his sails. He said that the banker's friend was where he himself aspired to be within a year, but that now he was sitting with nearly half of his twenty houses vacant. Mike shook his head. He couldn't take on that kind of risk, he said, for it would take him down financially. I agreed it didn't look very promising. I asked Mike what he had planned for the afternoon.

Mike laid out his plans to go to Wachovia Bank at two o'clock. He would call the Century 21 Realtor again and then he would drop by the HUD project and see what they charged for rents. Mike was launched, if not on an actual project, at least on the process—dealing with the municipality, attempting to secure financing, checking out the market to see if he should proceed. With what he learned from the banker, the question was, should he even get involved in real estate in Arcadia? Mike left for town, and I went back to bed.

I had confronted risky projects time after time in my career but had never doubted our market. Whatever I had built, had rented. This was new territory. I couldn't in good conscience advise Mike to proceed with the 519 renovation if there was no rental market.

At the end of the day, Mike returned. He was even more discouraged. The Wachovia banker had no authority to negotiate a foreclosure. All of that was done in Tampa. He'd simply have to submit an offer through the Realtor. The banker had asked Mike how much equity he had in his house, and Mike stretched a bit and told him he could commit $10,000 to the project. The banker told him they would lend against the purchase price of the house, but probably not against all the renovation costs of a new project in this market. He would have to find additional funds for the renovation.

Mike had gone over to the new low-income housing project. They were offering new apartments for $500 for a one-bedroom, $550 for a two-bedroom, $600 for a three-bedroom, and $650 for a four-bedroom, and they still had half the complex to fill. That explained why there were so many vacancies elsewhere in the town. Every landlord in this small community was facing intense competition from the new subsidized project.

Mike had pegged his pricing correctly at $650 for a four-bedroom, two-bath and suggested that not everybody would want to live in a low-income housing complex. Someone might prefer a single-family house close to the schools.

Perhaps he should go ahead and submit an offer through the Realtor. Set the price where he thought it should be for the house—maybe as low as $10,000. Write the narrative for his business plan. He could submit pictures of all the defects along with it and urge the bankers to come and see the house. He should explain to them that 519 N. Arcadia would simply continue to decline until it was worth nothing, unless a knowledgeable buyer such as Mike were to take it on and renovate it. Although it was doubtful that with a city full of foreclosures on their hands, the bankers would even care about visiting such a small project, but it was worth a try, plus it would give Mike the experience of preparing a written financing proposal for a bank.

Mike agreed that it would be better for the bank to get something on their money rather than just writing it off altogether. I encouraged him to explain that to them. This was a small project, but with his skills as a contractor, Mike was the right guy for the job. There was not a lot of upside, but it was worth submitting an offer. They were asking $39,900. He could show them, with the spreadsheet, why it was worth no more than $10,000. You never know, they might take it. I also encouraged Mike to pursue the East Magnolia properties, because at the end of that deal, he would have ten or twelve units for a year's worth of work. With the 519 deal, although it would be good experience for him, he would have one unit for his work.

The real question on the East Magnolia property was whether he would be able to rent ten or twelve new units on the market in Arcadia, or even just one. It was a dilemma.

Carol and I would be leaving the next day, but we suggested that Mike go to see the mayor, the city planner, and the chamber of commerce. He should ask them about the demographics of the area. Were people indeed moving away? What were the statistics? Did anyone have a plan for improving economic conditions in the area? It was unlikely in this small town, but someone might. It would be good to see if what the banker had said was true. He should get a feel for what was going on locally. A rental property can look good on paper, but it exists within an entire community. Mike was confident he could do the renovation work and management on either of the properties we had looked at, but his success would be dependent on market forces outside his control. Was there a market? He should call the banker back and ask him how to get in touch with his friend with the twenty units and eight vacancies. It would be good for him to meet other landlords in the area and get their take on the local rental market.

We talked it over and agreed he might be better off buying in Port Charlotte or somewhere along the coast. Maybe there would be a stronger rental market there. Also, tomorrow he should go and see the Realtor again for the East Magnolia properties. There might be a market for apartments in those buildings—more of an upscale market. Underneath all the dirt and debris around them, these properties had a distinctive elegance with their Spanish architecture. They were well located in a highly visible area, and if there were any market at all at the upper end, these might be his best bet.

Above all, I told Mike, he shouldn't give up his desire to own property. No one could take the desire away from him, and by holding on to his desire to create an independent income in real estate, opportunities would eventually open up. Hold on to your desires, and opportunities would appear in the most unexpected places. I guaranteed that to him.

Mike appreciated my encouragement. He said he had gotten pretty discouraged after being so high on the possibilities this past weekend. Carol and I reassured him something would open up.

We had to leave for New York the next day. On the drive

to the Fort Myers Airport, I told her it would be really lovely to stay a while and see what Mike comes up with.

She pointed out that I had given Mike the tools to find and analyze a rental property. It would be up to him to move forward on it. It had to be his project, however it turned out. She was right. With the easy credit of the past decade or so, the Florida real estate market had overheated. Indeed, the real estate market for the entire country had overheated. Property prices had inflated far beyond what their worth would have been had their value been based on what they would rent for, or what someone could pay assuming more normal interest rates. Values were falling, and while this would be painful for many, for others it would become an opportunity to buy, to renovate, and to create the beginnings of an independent income in real estate. The question in Arcadia and for Mike was whether the property would rent at all based on the economic climate.

Carol suggested that we leave him on his own for a while and see what he might come back with. Again, she was right. Doing his research and waiting for the market to come back might be the wisest decision for Mike at the moment. I had never experienced a collapsed market. Holding on to his desire to own property was the important thing, that, and waiting for the market to come back. At some point, it had to come from him. Mike would have to make the decision to jump into it on his own, or not. No one could do it for him.

CHAPTER 6

WHY CREDIT WORKS:
Borrowing to Become Wealthy

Once the obstacles to action have been removed,
anxious hesitation is a mistake that is bound to bring
disaster, because one misses one's opportunity.

At fourteen, my father told me it was time to set up a checking account. I would earn my allowance monthly, deposit it into my checking account, and pay for what I needed by check. It all seemed fine to me, until it came time to balance the darned thing. It took a few arduous sessions with my dad, but after learning the process, all went well.

Sitting with me explaining the system, my dad had told me that writing a check is based on trust. There is no inherent value in that piece of paper. The only value a check has, he told me, was someone's trust in you that you had the funds in your account and would honor payment. That seems pretty obvious to me now. It was a new concept at age fourteen. He had just taught me that our trust in one another is the basis of all our financial transactions.

With that in mind, with the millions of dollars borrowed over the years, I have never missed a payment, never even been late on a mortgage payment. People learn to trust you based on you honoring your word. A check, a note, a mortgage are all instruments promising you will pay what you say you will pay—that there is value there to back them up. Keep your word, and people will stand in line to lend you money. The bankers will call on you to borrow money from them. Break your word, and they will shun you like the plague.

In the mid-1960s, at the age of twenty-three, I attended a cocktail party in Nashville given by Jack Massey, a neighbor of my aunt. Mr. Massey had been the one to discover Colonel Sanders. He purchased the name and the rights to a few Kentucky Fried Chicken stores that Colonel Sanders had begun, and he had turned it into an international franchise. He befriended me that evening on his veranda and told me that the happiest day of his life was when he came home and told his wife that he owed a million dollars. He must have seen my quizzical expression, because he paused to let his words sink in. He added then, that if he owed a million dollars, it proved that he must be worth it! And he finished off with a belly laugh.

It was impossible not to share his enthusiasm there on the veranda. But it was a different concept for me. You owe a million dollars, so you must be worth a million dollars? Slowly, it began to sink in.

The underlying assumption is that if someone lends you a million dollars, they trust that you have the assets, either tangible in the way of property, or intangible such as an idea, or a design, or a plan to earn money, that make you worth a million dollars. Years later, I realized that Mr. Massey's words have had a huge impact on me. It was all right to borrow money. Just like my checking account at age fourteen, it is based on trust, and borrowing money can even make you wealthy!

How does it work, that borrowing money can make you wealthy? This is not an original concept. As you will see in the table that follows, it is simply a fact that if you save $1,000 and put it in the bank, you will earn whatever interest the bank is paying. Rates may vary but let's say that at the end of a year, you will have earned 2%, or 3%, or even 5% in additional money depending on what rate of interest your bank is paying on your savings account. Your $1,000 will be worth $1,020 at 2% annually, $1,030 at 3%, and $1,050 at 5%. Certainly, it is prudent to save. And the longer you keep the money in the bank, the more it grows, due to compound interest.

Bank Savings Account	
$1,000 @ Annual Interest	
2%	$20
3%	$30
5%	$50

As shown in the next table, at the end of ten years, compounded annually at 2% it would be worth $1,219. At 3% it would be worth $1,344, and at 5% $1,629. Some banks even calculate the interest daily, which would yield a slightly higher annual rate—you get the idea.

Assume a $1,000 Deposit in your Personal Savings Account										
$1,000 Year 1	2	3	4	5	6	7	8	9	10	TOTAL
Interest										
2% $20.00	$20.40	$20.81	$21.22	$21.65	$22.08	$22.52	$22.97	$23.43	$23.90	$218.99
3% $30.00	$30.90	$31.83	$32.78	$33.77	$34.78	$35.82	$36.90	$66.90	$96.90	$430.56
5% $50.00	$52.50	$55.13	$57.88	$60.78	$63.81	$67.00	$70.36	$73.87	$77.57	$628.89

Assume for a moment that instead of putting your $1,000 into a savings account at a bank, you use it as a down payment to purchase an asset (say a small house) worth $10,000. And assume that the value of this $10,000 house grows by 2%, 3%, or 5% annually. At the end of the first year at 2%, your asset would now be worth $10,200; at 3%, $10,300; at 5%, $10,500, because at 2% you would have realized $200 on your original $1,000; at 3%, $300; at 5%, $500.

Look what this does to your original cash. The $1,000 you invested originally is now worth $1,200, $1,300, or $1,500. How much did you earn on your money? At 2% you earned $200/$1,000 = 20% on your original cash; at 3% you earned $300/$1,000 = 30%; at 5% you earned $500/$1,000 = 50%; and if you were able to earn 10%, you earned $1,000/$1,000 = 100%. If you were able earn 5% for two years you would have earned $1,000 or double your money! If you were able to earn 10% on the larger asset for a single year, you would double your original amount of money!

Assume $1,000 Controls a $10,000 Property		
$1,000		**% Return on Original $1,000**
2% on $10,000	$200	20%
3% on $10,000	$300	30%
5% on $10,000	$500	50%
10% on $10,000	$1,000	**100% (your $1,000 has doubled!)**

Consider for a moment that you can earn 5% on the $10,000 asset. You do it for two years. You earn $500 each year. At the end of that time you have doubled your original $1,000 to $2,000. With that $2,000 you control an asset worth $20,000, which is to say you have put 10% down ($2,000 equity) to control an asset (let's say a building) worth $20,000. You make repairs, you reconfigure the layout to gain an additional bedroom, the property appreciates; however it happens, your $20,000 house grows in value by 5% a year, or this time $1,000 per year.

At the end of two years you will have $2,000 more dollars, or $4,000 total. You sell the house or refinance it and take out your $4,000. With that money as 10% down, you control an asset worth $40,000. It grows at 5% a year. 5% times $40,000 = $2,000, so at the end of two more years you have $4,000 more dollars or $8,000 total. And so it goes: From $1,000—your original amount; to $2,000—transaction one; to $4,000—transaction two; to $8,000—transaction three; to $16,000—transaction four; to $32,000—transaction five; to $64,000—transaction six; to $128,000—transaction seven; to $256,000—transaction eight; to $512,000—transaction nine; to $1,024,000—transaction ten. It's a geometric progression, doubling your equity with each transaction!

By using your original $1,000, and controlling a building worth ten times as much, by gaining the appreciation or growth in value on the building valued at ten times as much as your original asset, by selling each time your equity doubles, in ten transactions, your original $1,000 will be worth over $1,000,000. Compare this with the $1,629 you would have if you had simply put it in a savings account for ten years. **This is the power of leveraging borrowed money to create a fortune for yourself.**

Notice how your Equity Doubles with each Transaction

Beginning Cash: Transaction	1	2	3	4	5	6	7	8	9	Equity after 10th Transaction
Equity $1,000	$2,000	$4,000	$8,000	$16,000	$32,000	$64,000	$128,000	$256,000	$512,000	**$1,024,000**
Controls $10,000	$20,000	$40,000	$80,000	$160,000	$320,000	$640,000	$1,280,000	$2,560,000	$5,120,000	**$10,240,000**
10% Earned on Controlled amount $1,000	$2,000	$4,000	$8,000	$16,000	$32,000	$64,000	$128,000	$256,000	$512,000	**$1,024,000**
New Equity Amount $1,000	$2,000	$4,000	$8,000	$16,000	$32,000	$64,000	$128,000	$256,000	$512,000	**$1,024,000**

103

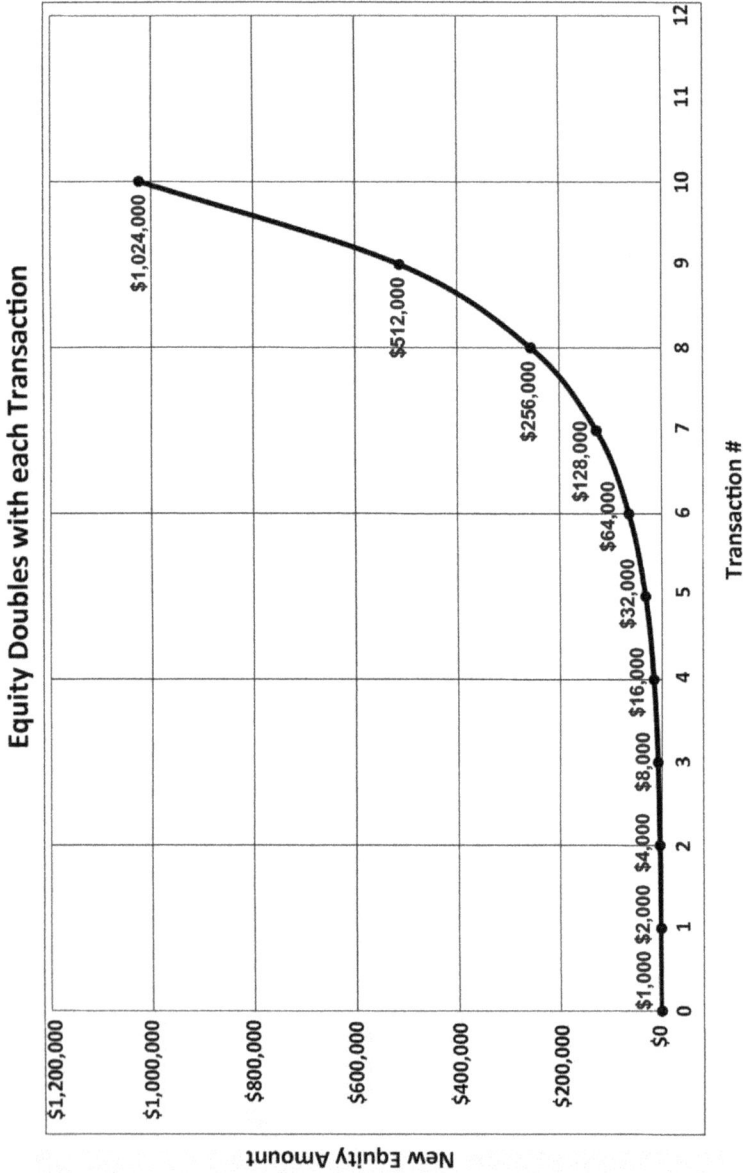

When I first read this principle in William Nickerson's book, *How I Turned $1,000 into a Million in Real Estate in my Spare Time*, I could hardly believe it. His book was first published in 1958, and is long out of print, but the basic premise is sound. He was writing for a market in California in boom times after World War II, but the same idea will work for you in your community, however large or small.

The power of credit is the engine that drives our economy. It was no more evident than in 2008, when banks stopped lending. The governments world-wide leapt to the rescue, infusing cash back into the economy, guaranteeing loans between banks, whatever they could do to attempt to assure that credit would continue to function. Without credit, business comes to a halt.

Let me give you an example of what lack of credit means in an economy. In 1993, I took a business trip to mainland China. A good friend of mine owned a facility in northern Pennsylvania that manufactured structural wall panels. He had been contacted by a representative of the Chinese government to come to China to explore the possibility of establishing a joint venture, teaching the Chinese the technology for building the wall panels for use in inexpensive housing. My friend printed a business card for me and invited me along as chairman of his board of directors. Our host and guide was a graduate student at Harvard. Our itinerary was set well in advance, and we would be visiting areas of the country where we were told a Caucasian had never been. We drove through the countryside in a Mercedes with an armed guard in the front seat and flags on the front fenders.

Premier Deng Xiaoping had established five economic

development zones in China at the time. In this communist country in 1993, these were experiments in capitalism. Private-property ownership of a sort was allowed in these areas; lending was allowed, and these zones were flourishing with new industry and construction. Where people could borrow money and reap the rewards of their efforts, the economy flourished. The Premier was beginning to see the power of capitalism and was inviting scores of Western enterprises to China to establish joint ventures. We visited Shanghai and saw forty-story skyscrapers being built, surrounded with forty stories of bamboo scaffolding! We visited Haikou, an island off the coast in the south near Vietnam and saw chemical factories and manufacturing plants. From all appearances, his experiments in capitalism were definitely a success. We spoke with Communist Party representatives in various locations around the country to show them my friend's concept for inexpensive housing and, in a few cases, to negotiate tentative deals.

Driving for hours through the countryside, we came upon countless partially built houses. One house had a foundation, another had walls halfway constructed. Another had the roof on, but all had obviously been under construction for extended periods. Weeds grew up on the sites. Construction debris lay around. No one was working. I turned and asked our guide why so many buildings were left unfinished.

He explained that China was a communist country. There was no credit in China. If a farmer wants to build a house for his family, he explained to us, the farmer works; he saves; he pours the footer for the building. He will work a little more and earn the money for a concrete block, and then another one. It may take him twenty years to build the house, but at the end of twenty years, he will own it. And where will the farmer live in the meantime? Our guide said that the farmer and his family will live with his parents.

I turned back and watched the countryside go by—poor and underdeveloped. There was no credit in China. There was no trust. I compared it to how this scenario would have unfolded at home. A young couple would have saved enough money for a down payment on a house, or their parents would have assisted them perhaps. They would borrow the rest of the money they needed from a bank. They would build or buy their house and move in with their children. At the end of twenty years, they too would own their house, but during those twenty years, they certainly had not been living with their parents. They would have been comfortable in their own home. Furthermore, multiply that one house they lived in by another million homes a year being constructed, most of them financed on credit—you begin to see the economy thriving, as industry produces the construction vehicles and equipment, the timber and concrete, the wiring and plumbing, the roofing and siding, the appliances, the carpets, and furniture for each one of those homes that were financed on credit. Trust and credit are a wonderful thing.

My friend and I had sat in local Communist Party assemblies, negotiating deals through an interpreter, but nothing was ever finalized. Everything was left amorphous and up in the air. It was if we were going through the motions for some unknown reason. We didn't know if we had a deal or not. They seemed to be simply picking our brains.

A few weeks after we returned to the United States, our

guide from Harvard, who had helped set up the trip original-ly, called my friend and asked him if he had actually signed any contracts. My friend told him that he had not. The guide paused and commented that that was odd, because he had just found out that the Communist Party chief in one of the towns we visited had taken a signed contract to the authori-ties to prove that they had been productive in meeting their quotas for joint ventures. It had my friend's signature on it.

As he recounted this story to me, my friend and I had to laugh. Here was one more incident of lack of trust. We could see why there was no credit in China—essentially there was no trust. We hoped all those foreign firms trying to do busi-ness in China realize who and what they are dealing with at that time. The Chinese certainly have a different value sys-tem than ours.

Assuming the honesty and integrity of the borrower and the lender, credit is a powerful engine for economic growth for an individual and, indeed, for an entire nation. It can be a powerful engine for your personal economic growth as well. You should welcome the chance to borrow money, provided you can put it to use making more. This is totally different from borrowing to buy a car, or to take a trip, or for living ex-penses. And as we all know, too much credit card debt at 20% interest can get us into trouble. Borrowing to purchase an income property, if properly done with discipline, can be the beginning of growing a fortune for yourself and your family.

CHAPTER 7

FINDING YOUR FIRST PROPERTY:
Stop Worrying About the Money

---

*If an individual is bent only on pleasures
and enjoyment, it is easy for him to lose his sense
of the limits that are necessary.*

It's time for you to look for your first property. You have the desire. How will you find it? Where should it be? What size should it be? In an afternoon of driving around, Mike and I had located five properties that were good possibilities. Some were listed with a Realtor; some just looked interesting due to their location and the potential for developing them from large single-family homes into multi-family units. We had gotten into the car and gone looking. You can do the same. Walk, ride a bicycle, ride a bus. Go around the area and see what looks intriguing to you. Look in the newspaper. Is anything listed as "For Sale by Owner"? Are there any income properties listed with a Realtor? Ask your friends. Is anyone you know in the rental business? Ask them. It won't take long for you to find and identify one or more properties for sale.

First of all, stop worrying about the money, even if you don't have any to spare or you don't think you have enough to buy a property. Or maybe you do have money saved, or inherited, or you have a rich and sympathetic uncle. Whatever the case, money is a tool; it is not a roadblock. It is not the barrier that stands between you and real estate acquisition. The only thing that stands between you and acquiring your first property, provided you have the desire, is time and perseverance.

You have been shopping. You have found a house or an apartment complex that you like. What do you do now? If it is not listed for sale through a Realtor, contact the owner. As Mike and I did in Arcadia, you can find the owner either at the county assessor's office or online at the assessor's website. If for some reason it is not listed there, try the county clerk's office. Every property in a municipality is listed—the deed is recorded. You can also go to the local building department at your city hall and ask to see the file at the address of your property. All of this is a matter of public record. You can also go to the property and knock on the door, ask who owns the property. It can be that simple to find the right person to talk to.

Once you have found the owner, call them up. Tell them that you drove by their property and were really intrigued by it. Ask if they have considered selling it. You will get back one of three answers: "Yes." "No." "Maybe." There may be many permutations of these, but basically that is what you will get. Realtors and principals contact me regularly about my willingness to sell a property. It's part of the business. Muster up your courage and make that initial contact.

It may take a few properties and a few calls, but eventually you will find someone interested in selling their house or apartment building. If this is your first foray into the field, I recommend that you start with residential properties. We all understand the basics of renting and living in a house or an apartment. A retail space or office suite presents a more specialized challenge. You're dealing with merchants or professionals who typically don't want to have their time wasted. Wait until you have an understanding of the basics and the confidence in your ability to purchase a residential property before you tackle a commercial property.

A Realtor will ask you how much money you have to put down. Think about your sources of funds. If you absolutely had to, how much money could you raise? Would your parents be able to lend you $1,000, $10,000, or more? Would a friend lend you money for a year or so? Have you saved anything? Do you have a life insurance policy you can borrow against? Can you imagine yourself in partnership with someone who has money? Whatever the amount you can conjure up, say it.

Or you can simply say that you don't think the money will be a problem and ask the Realtor if they have anything in the way of a duplex, a four-family house, or larger one that the numbers really work on. Your goal is to get inside a property, look it over, and get the income and expense numbers, to see if you can make money on the deal. A Realtor can be very helpful. If they are experienced with income property, they will help you with the analysis of the numbers. They can recommend which banks might be receptive to lending on the project. You could even ask if the seller is willing to take back paper on the sale (i.e., would they hold a second mortgage, thereby enabling you to buy the property with no cash of your own?).

It's important to develop a professional persona, and you can practice this in front of a mirror. Rehearse what you will say to a Realtor and a banker on the phone or in their office. How will you ask for financing on the project? How will you ask the seller to hold a second mortgage? I have found my acting background a great help in business; when I first began dealing in the world of banks and sellers and attorneys, it helped to rehearse in front of a mirror to create the confidence to make a presentation. It is not unlike creating a character on stage. This character, the one in front of the mirror, has the confidence to borrow money and buy a piece of property. It has the intelligence and is confident to be able to raise the money, or even negotiate a deal that won't require cash. You can blow it in front of a mirror without making a total fool of yourself.

It's not unheard of, once you have made contact with a seller, and once they know you, for them to agree to hold a second mortgage for the difference between the purchase price and what the bank will lend. It is something I have done dozens of times. It doesn't hurt to ask them, and in any case, if they won't hold all of it, maybe they will hold part of it in a second mortgage in order to make the sale. If they will, that will reduce the amount of cash you will need to come up with. In some cases, it could mean you don't have to come up with any cash at all.

My own trajectory followed something like this:

Property 1—a single-family home that the seller sold to me for simply taking over his monthly mortgage payment. Renovated it into a duplex thereby increasing the value, and refinanced it at a higher mortgage amount, allowing me to take out $5,000 in cash.

Property 2—a duplex. Used the $5,000 from property

1 as a down payment and borrowed an additional $5,000 against property 2 to renovate and add two bedrooms. With the additional value created from the increased rental income, borrowed another $5,000 and bought my next building.

Property 3—the duplex next door.

Property 4—found a dump down the street for $16,000. No money down. A buddy and I bought it together and each agreed to put up $5,000 to pay for the renovation. Buddy leaves for Mexico without ponying up his half. Buddy returns from Mexico. After a conversation with my attorney, buddy feels remorseful and gives me his half interest for $1. Through with buddies for a while.

Property 5—six-unit house for $30,000. Sell Property 4 for a profit and put money down on Property 5. Renovate and add two bedrooms. Upgrade and increase value. Wait a year and sell for $60,000. Buy a new car with the profit and look for next project.

Property 6—another six-unit property near the university. My dad lends me $6,000. Buy it for $49,000. Renovate and manage it for a couple of years along with my other properties and sell it for $75,000. Pay back my dad and move on to the next one.

And so it goes. Up to this point, I had spent probably five years buying, renovating, and selling. With my first property, it became apparent to me that I could be more effective making the deals rather than doing the renovations myself, so I began hiring help and supervising them early mornings before work, during my lunch hour, and after work.

But back to buying property. You see that after obtaining my first property and renovating it to create additional value, and borrowing against that value, it was possible without selling each one, to buy a second, third, fourth, and so on. Alternatively, I could have renovated each property, sold it, and taken the profits to purchase the next one. Either way, significant value was created from the renovations and general appreciation, and that "equity" was used to expand my holdings—this was only the beginning.

There is nothing keeping you from doing this too. Beg, borrow, save, or scrounge that first down payment! Refinance your house. Ask your dad or your grandmother. Put it on your credit card, if necessary. Make sure the property is one that will appreciate enough in value, either because it is rundown and you will renovate it, or because it is somewhat funky, and you can add rooms or redesign it to create more income. Don't be in a hurry, but purchase, renovate, hold long enough through a rental season or two to make sure the value is there, and then either sell or refinance to raise enough money for your next acquisition.

It is not a complicated formula, and you will be on your way with each property, and the cash flow generated monthly, toward creating an independent income in real estate.

CHAPTER 8

THE KEY TO SUCCESS IS MANAGEMENT:
Maximize the Value

If he gives himself over to extravagance,
he will have to suffer the consequences
with accompanying regret.

With the purchase of your first property, you have taken a big step. You have figured out how to assemble the purchase price with a combination of your own money or borrowed cash for a down payment. Possibly you have negotiated seller financing for part of the cost, and most likely a local bank has lent you the money for the balance of the purchase price, securing their position with a first mortgage. You have learned how to collect the rents and how to pay the bills.

You will have found that it is not unlike running your personal finances, and certainly it is the same principle of depositing money in the bank (or under the mattress,) and paying the expenses by check (or cash)—only now there are more of them. You will have added up the income monthly, whether it is from one unit, thirty units, or more. You will have subtracted the taxes, insurance, utilities, management, and maintenance costs, and if you have planned it carefully, there will be money left for you each month. You may have had to learn how to collect the rent from the slow payers—a call in the early evening, or a drop by on Saturday morning.

Not Sunday, and not after 8:00 p.m., for you cannot legally make dunning calls to those who owe you money after 8:00 p.m. nor on Sundays, at least not in New York State.

By now, you may have learned how to place advertising in your local paper, on the internet, or to post notices of "Apartment Available" in the local Laundromat. You have learned how to show an apartment to prospective tenants. You may have inherited one or more leases from the previous owner, and you may have used that as the agreement between you, as landlord, and your renter, as tenant. You may have gone to your local stationery store and purchased a standard legal form of a lease. (See Appendix B for a Sample Lease Agreement) Developing an appropriate lease agreement for your particular market, and your particular State's laws is an important part of the equation. You can talk to other landlords and ask to see theirs. You can talk to your attorney and have him/her develop one. Or you can go online and probably find one on the website of a local landlord. Be careful adapting it, and make sure it addresses your particular needs. Whatever you do, be sure to have a written, legally binding agreement between yourself and the tenant. Try to make it for a minimum of one year—people are accustomed to that as a standard, at least in our area. There may be instances when you need to write a month-to-month lease or shorter than a year, to accommodate a tenant's need to relocate. A point to note is that if the tenant is in the military, they have the right to break the lease if reassigned.

Realize there is no inherent value in bricks and mortar. *The key to success in real estate is management.* You, or someone you hire, will have to rent out your property, service the tenants, make them happy and satisfied with your building, and make them happy with you as a landlord. Someone will have to pay the bills on time and see to daily maintenance and capital improvements, such as a new roof, heating system or furniture. Only proper management maximizes the value of an income property.

From a financial standpoint, management doesn't have to be a hugely sophisticated endeavor. The charts, budgets, and schedules Mike and I developed earlier can be done with a pencil and legal pad. You don't have to master computerized bookkeeping before you can buy and manage an income property. You need only the basics, mentioned before—you have to be able to add and subtract, and you have to be able to talk to people to rent the units. And you need perseverance. Those are the skills you need. With practice, you will get better at all of it. The rest will become apparent as you go—managing your property and making sure the income exceeds the outgo.

How many properties can you manage on your own? It was possible for me, working evenings and weekends to handle about sixteen apartment units in four or five buildings. It required help to renovate them, but once they were rented in their new configuration, at the new rents, I could take care of the minor maintenance issues, repair the leaky faucets, cut the lawns, move furniture, turn over vacant units, and prepare them for new tenants on my own. At first, hiring a part-time assistant to handle the maintenance calls and do the repairs, was a luxury, but with expansion, it became a necessity. I wanted a life of my own too, apart from taking care of other people's needs.

At first, I handled all the rentals myself, taking the calls at home or at work and doing the showings after work or on the weekends. Gradually it became necessary to hire assistance with the day to day operations. While other people can rent the apartments for you, you must pay attention to see they are doing the job properly and that the money winds up in your pocket—not in theirs. Certainly, hire other people as needed, but remain in charge of your own staff and management.

The following story tells you why I feel so strongly about managing your own properties. In the 1970s, early in my real estate career, I met an interesting fellow and his girlfriend who had recently moved to Ithaca from California. He dressed in Bermuda shorts, wild shirts, and outrageously oversized sunglasses with yellow rims. In conservative Ithaca, he cut quite a figure. On the other hand, I was just learning to wear neckties and jackets to go to the bank. He had sold a few properties he owned in California and had come east with a great deal of money. I hadn't seen him for a few weeks, until one day we met again as he was walking out of the bank quite happy with himself, still dressed in shorts, a wild shirt, and his outrageous sunglasses. With a wide grin, he told me he had just closed on sixteen houses. I congratulated him and wished him well.

Being only on my third or fourth property at that time, I couldn't help but envy him. Each one had been a stretch, but somehow I had managed to find the money.

Several years later, I was sitting in a restaurant next to the canal that leads out into Cayuga Lake. It was a beautiful sunny day, there were ducks on the water and a slight breeze. When the waitress arrived, it was a shock to see that it was the girlfriend of my rich California friend. Introducing myself and masking my surprise at seeing her waiting tables, I asked how she was, and then how her boyfriend was. She looked at me and shook her head. He had left town. It turned out he had given over the management of his properties to a local management company and hadn't paid sufficient attention to what was happening. They had run them into the ground, and he had lost them all. They had broken up a while back, and here she was waiting tables.

I commiserated with her, for he had been a colorful figure, and she obviously cared for him; it was at that point I decided the only way to grow my own real estate portfolio was to *manage every property myself.* The key to creating value and success in real estate is management, and no one will give your properties the same care and attention that you will.

This is not to say that you cannot hire a reputable management company to manage your properties, you can. They will probably charge between 6% and 10% of the gross income. Many firms may charge a lower percentage to manage apartments, but then charge a fee for each lease they sign, and they may also run their own crews and charge for maintenance.

Whatever the model, the key is oversight. If you simply turn your properties over to a management company and fail to demand monthly accounting and accountability, there can be a tendency for a management company to get sloppy. They don't rent your units with the same dedication that you might. There is simply no way they will be as motivated as you, the owner, will be, to see that your properties are fully rented, and the tenants properly cared for. The management company will collect a fee whether they do a first rate job or a mediocre job. You, on the other hand, will have the mortgage to pay, and if it is not paid by the rents, you will have to pay it from some other source. That can be painful. If you hire a management company, pay attention to their performance just as you would if you hire your own staff to assist you.

The same applies to service to your tenants. If you are not doing the hands-on work yourself, stop by now and then and talk to your tenants. Was the repair job done properly? Was it done on a timely basis? Were they satisfied? If not, take steps to correct that, whether it is with your own employees or the management company. You are the boss now and you have to pay attention!

There is another aspect of management that is extremely important. I had learned to be pretty successful at managing properties myself and hiring outside help now and then as needed—until an eighteen-year-old kid put his hand through a windowpane. He was painting the window trim on the exterior of my newly renovated house. Before he started, I had told him I didn't have insurance. He had said no problem and was just happy to have summer work helping with renovations. When he put his hand through the windowpane it nearly severed his right index finger. I heard about it that day and went up to see him in the hospital. He was going to be okay, but he would be out of work for a while.

A few weeks later, a legal summons arrived in the mail. It turned out his father was an attorney, and the summons directed that I appear in court the following week, for failing to carry Worker's Compensation Insurance on an employee.

I didn't even know what Worker's Compensation Insurance was. I found out soon enough.

There exists in New York State a manual that lists the value of every appendage and organ: your eyes, your teeth, and various other body parts. If you are an employee and lose the use of one of these while on the job, you are entitled to a certain dollar amount of compensation from Worker's Compensation Insurance. As I recall, an index finger was worth $1,500 at the time. If the person paying you does not have this insurance, unless you are a private contractor, it does not matter that he told you he didn't have insurance and that you agreed to work without it. The person paying you is obligated by state law to carry Worker's Compensation Insurance, and if he does not carry it, and you are injured on the job, your employer is liable for treble damages, plus your medical expenses, plus a fine from the state. There I was, sitting in court getting my education in how to run a business. It was an expensive lesson. My painter didn't lose his finger, but he took a while to recover, and I was assessed a fine, plus medical expenses totaling over $4,500.

The next day my attorney and I began the process of forming a corporation—and from that point on, whenever a new employee was hired, they were paid by my new corporation with Federal and State Income Tax, Disability Insurance, Social Security, all withheld, plus Worker's Compensation Insurance. The cost of having an employee skyrocketed by 35%, compared to paying them out of my pocket, but now I was legal and could at least sleep at night.

More than ever, I was determined to manage every property myself. My conversation in the restaurant on the canal had been providential. It was a clear direction for me to manage my properties myself. I was determined to grow my business, and while keeping financial records for each property in a separate set of books, all workers were paid through my new management company—Ithaca Rentals and Renovations, Inc. Each of my properties hired my management company. It would become the management arm of my growing business.

By then I had been at this for four years, owned six properties totaling twenty apartment units, and had hired a part-time maintenance assistant. I still rented all the units myself, and still maintained my full-time job at the local college.

Appendix B shows our basic lease. Note that we collect a security deposit, and in New York State, if you have more than six units in any one building, these deposits have to go into a savings account at the bank in the tenant's name, and the tenant must be paid the interest, less 1%, which the landlord may keep. Our lease and forms have been developed over the years; originally, they were written for a student market, but we have now adapted them for professionals, seniors, families, and now commercial tenants, as we have grown into those markets. You should pursue legal advice of our own, but this example of a lease will give you an idea of the basics to include in your own lease.

You can also access management information online from the Institute of Real Estate Management (IREM). IREM offers a series of courses on property management, which, if you continue expanding, you might find useful. Check your state's website. You can find information about tenant/landlord law online. Your local bookstore or library will also have books on the specifics and details of how to manage property. Our lease does cover the basic concerns between landlords and tenants, which we have experienced over the years. However, use it at your own risk and adapt it to your particular needs.

Your town, like mine, may have a landlord's association. Ours meets monthly and covers various management topics. Meeting other landlords and talking with them will expand your personal horizons and give you insights into the market that might otherwise take years of trial and error to learn.

Owning and renting property can be a private affair between you and the tenant but know that there is a whole body of law governing the transaction between the two parties—landlord and tenant. A lot of it is common sense, but you would be well advised to learn about such things as discrimination and the Fair Housing Act (you can't refuse to rent to a tenant because they have children, for instance), the tenant's right to privacy, when dunning calls can (and cannot) be made, landlord/tenant liability, and so on.

Just keep in mind that there is no inherent value in bricks and mortar, and that the key to success in real estate is management. You will make money, or not, based on keeping your properties full, your tenants happy, and your policies and procedures within the law.

CHAPTER 9

BUYING A PROBLEM WITH NO CASH:
Sweat Equity

He must not lay the blame on others.

You may still be feeling stymied by how to raise enough money to buy your first property. The following are two examples of buying properties without putting up any cash. In an area of our town near Cornell University, there are streets filled with old houses, many of which used to be the homes of Cornell professors. Today these houses are filled with students. In the 1970s, many of these structures were in a state of disrepair from overuse and lack of reinvestment by the owners. One of them, a lovely three-story white brick row house on Eddy Street, had a fire. No one was hurt, but the beautiful gabled roof was burned off. The tenants lost their apartments, and the owner lost a good investment he had owned for years.

The house sat vacant, open to the elements, for the better part of a year. Driving by one day, I had the thought that it might be possible to own that house. Asking around, I found that the owner was a Mr. Petrillose, who also owned a string of laundries and Johnny's Big Red Grill, one of the favorite restaurants and watering holes for Cornell students. I went to the restaurant one afternoon and asked to see Mr. Petrillose. The bartender said he was out and would be back in the evening, and the best time to see him, he told me, was after the restaurant closed at 10:00 p.m.

That evening I went back and introduced myself to Mr. Petrillose and his wife. They appeared to be in their late seventies. They sat alone, eating dinner at a table in the restaurant and agreed I could join them. I asked about the burned-out building down on Eddy Street. Was it for sale? No it wasn't, but he asked who I was, and why I might want it. I told him I had renovated a number of houses in town and thought that if he would sell me his, for no money down, and subordinate to a first mortgage from the bank for the money needed to do the renovations, I might be able to renovate his burned-out house, and he might get some income from it, rather than it just sitting there vacant. He said he'd think about it, but it was highly unlikely. If I wanted to talk further, I could stop back at the restaurant in a couple of weeks.

Over the next couple of months, I went back to the restaurant several times after closing hours and sat and drank a beer with Mr. Petrillose and his wife while they ate their dinner. They took a liking to me. He told me he had checked up on me, and I had a reputation as a "doer." I asked to go through the building, and he simply handed me the keys. From my walk-through, it seemed there was a possibility of turning the three-story building into a series of townhouses with five bedrooms each. There could be two full townhouses; and in the remaining space, a three-bedroom, a two-bedroom, and a one-bedroom apartment.

Mr. Petrillose finally agreed to sell the building for $75,000, for which he would hold a second mortgage. He agreed to allow me to go to the bank and borrow up to $125,000 on a first mortgage to cover the cost of renovations. The bank would be in first position; Mr. Petrillose and his wife would be in second position. He told me he owned the building free and clear and had received his insurance money on the building in the amount of $24,000, so he didn't worry much about being in second position.

I prepared a plan for the bank, showing them how much the renovations would cost and how much income and expenses on the building would be once the work was done. My banker listened. He had seen each of my previous renovations, and he knew I could do the work. After running it by his credit committee, he agreed that the bank would lend against the building in first position so long as Mr. Petrillose would subordinate his loan in second place. We had a deal!

I was still working full-time at Ithaca College, but came by every morning before work to get the crews going and checked in again at lunch time and again after work. We installed a dumpster and began gutting the burned-out shell. The city building department reviewed my plans and issued a building permit to renovate the structure into a total of five apartments.

The local newspaper did a story on the project, and the caption on the photograph said, "Local real estate developer tackles burned-out row-house." I was a bit surprised but realized that's what I was—a real estate developer. I had never particularly thought of my role in the process, but the label seemed appropriate even though it was only a part-time job.

In spite of all the problems renovating a burned-out structure—I found out, for instance, that when mortar between the brick is subjected to intense heat from a building fire, it turns to sand, and the building inspector required that we re-lay the brick for the upper ten feet at the rear of the building where the fire had started—in spite of these problems, we finished the project well in advance of the next rental season, plus we had every unit pre-leased before the sheetrock was even on the walls. Students would stop in while we were working, and I rented every unit without placing a single ad in the student newspaper.

This success in the student rental market reaffirmed my conviction that by providing quality housing in a market that had been let go for so long, I would be financially successful. The bank was happy. Mr. and Mrs. Petrillose were happy. It had been possible to renovate a property that now produced over $800 a month for me and had cost me only the work of renovation. All the money for both the acquisition and the renovation of this three-story, white brick row house on Eddy Street had been borrowed, and I was happy. Buying a problem was the way to go. This convinced me more than ever that problems equal opportunities.

The second example began with a phone call later that fall. The Eddy Street property was up and running smoothly. My phone rang one evening. The voice of an older man said he wanted to make me a deal I couldn't refuse. I perked up but was a little skeptical. The man told me his attorney had recommended that he call me, and he mentioned the name of an attorney I had gotten to know in my real estate dealings. His attorney had told him about my renovation of the burned-out building on Eddy Street.

He proceeded to tell me about a fire he had had in a five-unit building on Quarry Street. He said he would like to offer me that building for nothing down. He would hold the purchase price in a second mortgage, allowing me to go to the bank and borrow enough to do the renovation. He also offered to sell me his six-unit building across the street as part of the package; I could do the renovation on the burned out property, and he would collect on the mortgages of both properties.

When someone offers me a deal I can't refuse, my tendency is to treat it like the used car salesman selling me someone else's problem. But I had done this before, and this fellow sounded genuine. I was still working at the college, so we made arrangements to meet at the properties the following day during my lunch hour.

When hardwood floors are soaked by water from a fire hose and left open to the elements, they tend to do amazing things. We walked into the living room on the first floor of the Quarry Street property and saw a maze of twisted lumber that shot off the floor at different angles, some boards reaching nearly to the ceiling, others twisting around themselves like the structure of DNA. I had never seen anything like it. After the fire, the rains had poured in and soaked the entire building for what must have been months. The Eddy Street building had been nothing like this.

We worked out the financial transaction there in the living room among the twisted flooring. I would buy both buildings, a total of eleven units. The six units across the street were full and functioning. This building would need a total gut and renovation. He would sell them both for $125,000, and I could go to the bank and borrow up to $150,000 to renovate the burned-out building. He would subordinate to a first mortgage on both properties.

Here was what is known as a "willing seller." He was older and retired, and he no longer wanted to face the work of owning apartments, particularly after the fire. It was simply overwhelming for him to face the problem of how to rebuild his apartment building.

My attorney drew up the purchase offer, which outlined the terms of purchase for both properties. I hired a Cornell architecture student who drew up the new layout, including a two-story atrium in the living room of the townhouses that would be constructed. The bank again agreed to lend based on the completed ("as-built") value of the project. The risk was whether the work could be completed, and the apartments rented; however, with each project the process and the risk had become more manageable in my mind. Again, the leases for the renovated burned-out building were signed before the next rental season, even before the work was completed. My net monthly income increased by nearly $1,000.

Let me give you another example of buying a problem with no personal cash. Recently, a fellow who used to work as one of my maintenance superintendents, called me about a house located near the university. It had been rented to students. It had experienced a fire but was not beyond repair. For nearly a year, it had sat vacant. He had the thought to buy it, renovate it, and rent it again to students. It was a large duplex with five bedrooms on each side. He didn't have much money, but he told me he and his wife had good credit.

He asked if I would recommend him to the loan officer at the bank. He had negotiated with the seller to hold a second mortgage while he did the reconstruction. He had projected the income and expenses for the project as though it were completed, and at the end of renovation, once rented, there would be enough value for the bank to put a conventional first mortgage on the property that would cover repaying the seller the original cost of purchase plus the cost of the renovations.

His equity in the project would be the work he had done to rebuild it—his sweat equity—and for that he would also be paid from the loan proceeds. In other words, he had estimated the cost of construction and included the cost of materials and his own labor to do the job. He would be paid by the project for doing the work of renovation, as well as owning it at the end.

This man had always been honest and hard-working when he had worked for me, and I agreed to recommend him to the bank with the suggestion that he put his proposal to the bank in writing. He did, and together we edited it. The bank agreed to his plan.

A year later, after a lot of work on his part, he and his wife owned a newly renovated duplex with five bedrooms on each side without their having put any of their own money into the project. He had restored an eyesore in the community. He had rented the two units to student groups, and they had added nearly $1,000 a month to their income for as long as they owned and managed the building.

The neighborhood was happy to be rid of an eyesore and a hazard. The bank was happy, for they could point to this project as one they had financed for the benefit of the community. And my former employee was happy, for he had identified a problem, solved it, and was now reaping the rewards. All he had to go on initially was his desire to increase his income and financial security—to create an independent income in real estate.

CHAPTER 10

AN INCREMENT OF A LIFETIME INCOME:
Each Deal Adds to It

Only when we realize that our mistakes
are of our own making will such disagreeable
experiences free us of error.

By the end of the 1970s, I had mustered enough courage and had enough stable income from my properties to leave the security of the college and start my own film business making industrial and sales films for local and regional clients. Between filmmaking and my apartments, I hoped to be able to eke out a living.

Filmmaking was an arduous process—finding a client who needed a sales tool to promote a product; selling them on my ability to produce their film; meeting with their marketing people and then writing the script. It often required travel to various locations around the country to shoot the film. Back, in my modest studio in Ithaca, I would edit the film, take it to the client's office for review, make changes, and finally deliver a finished 16mm film. The entire process for a ten-to fifteen-minute sales piece would take four to six months. Next step—find another client and repeat the process. It was satisfying, made enough money for me to live on, and I did it for three years—sell, write, shoot, edit, correct, deliver, and repeat the process.

As much as I enjoyed my independence and the variety of the film business, I came to the realization that if I were to put the same energy and time it took making a film into real estate, each deal made would be *creating an increment of a lifetime income.* My job making sales films, would require schlepping six hundred pounds of film gear around the country shooting salt mines, medical sterilizers, and gravel pits for the rest of my life (this was before portable digital technology). My crates of 16mm equipment with lights, tape recorders and sound equipment, tripods, and still cameras took huge physical effort to move from location to location, and although I occasionally hired an assistant to help me schlep, it was a one-man shop.

In real estate, my first house, had made $100 a month free and clear. Each additional house produced more monthly income. I figured by purchasing ten houses and have each one produce just $100 a month, it would be possible to give up my $8,000 a year salary at the college and retire.

Things worked out much better than originally projected, and I enjoyed making money from the properties. Making a film was a creative process. Renovating a house was a creative process, certainly in a different way, but finding a property, making the deal with the seller and the banks, figuring out what was needed to improve the property, doing the work, and delivering it completed to a tenant was not so different from making a film and delivering it to a client.

Indeed, it was not that different from creating a role as an actor, rehearsing it for days and weeks on end, as I had done in college and summer stock theater, and finally delivering it to an audience on opening night. Now, the experience, realization, and understanding of the formula for purchasing a property, often without cash or with all borrowed cash, made sense to me. With each property, it was possible to add to an increment of a life time income—this thrust me into hyper-drive.

Borrowing money and doing it safely seemed to come naturally to me. So far, my income always exceeded my outgo. Now what was needed in order to grow, was capital. One could only go so far borrowing against one house to purchase another, and I was not interested in selling my hard-won apartment buildings in order to raise cash to build another. So far, I had purchased houses in the downtown area of Ithaca. With the two burned-out projects, I had moved into holdings closer to the university, and my strategy was evolving to create quality housing for students as close to the university as possible. The idea of creating an increment of a lifetime income in real estate with each purchase and renovation was expanding my vision and my audacity.

After renovating old buildings for seven years, I now owned thirty-five apartments in eight houses, and still had my film business. Each property had been purchased with borrowed funds. Now, at thirty-seven years old, and having done a variety of renovations including two burned-out shells, I wanted to grow.

I began driving around town, looking at vacant sites with the idea of constructing a new project from the ground up. The head of Cornell Real Estate was a gentleman named Jim Yarnell. Mr. Yarnell was from Maine. He told me a story of living in Maine and how the tourists would come through his town and remark on the horrible smell. The paper mill operated on the edge of town and sent plumes of sulfurous smoke into the air. He would laugh and deliver his usual response: "Smells like money to us!"

At this stage of my development, I realized that I had identified my market; student housing was not as glamorous perhaps as luxury apartments, shopping malls, and office buildings, but it was lucrative, and at least in our local market, it seemed a relatively safe way to begin.

Sitting in Mr. Yarnell's office one morning, I asked him if the university owned any properties in close proximity to campus they might consider selling. He bluntly informed me that Cornell never sold any property. I was instantly deflated. It had seemed like such a brainstorm to speak with the head of Cornell Real Estate about finding a site close to campus.

Then he paused, thought for a moment and said that the university did own a three-acre parcel across the street from the main campus. It had been given to the university as part of an estate. They had torn down the mansion that was on the site with the thought of using it for student housing someday. He said that they might sell that parcel. They didn't have any concrete plans for it, but if a student housing complex were to be built on it, then the university would have accomplished its purpose of improving the housing for students without having to do the work themselves.

I had a good idea which property it was, and asked Mr. Yarnell how much the university would sell it for. He looked through his records and thought for a moment. They would sell it for $125,000. Instinct kicked in—would he take less? He said that $125,000 was probably the number, and in any case, a sale of university land would have to be approved by the Board of Trustees.

I was floored. $125,000 was a fortune to me, and while the equity in my properties exceeded that amount, I had nowhere near that much cash. Managing to mask my chagrin, I told Mr. Yarnell he could expect a call from me in the near future and thanked him for taking the time to meet with me. "Good," he said. And he repeated that he thought they would sell me that parcel. That ended our meeting.

I was excited, but I didn't have that kind of cash, and didn't want to sell my existing properties in order to raise the purchase price of the land. The site was a good one, but the whole idea was speculative. My current properties, while not making me rich, had at least given me a certain financial security. The geometric progression of using other people's money to control assets larger than my meager funds would allow had worked for me, but I had neglected the step of selling each property to raise the equity for the next property. The security of owning many properties had gotten the best of me—the $2,000 to $4,000 to 8, 16, 32, 64, 128, 256, 512, and 1,024 was working. I was at about the $128,000 level, but had been able to do it by borrowing on one property to purchase the next, not by selling one to raise the money for the next one. Theoretically my return was infinite, since at that point none of my own money was invested.

It was 1980. My father had graduated from Cornell in 1940 with a degree in engineering. He had been an officer in the army in charge of ordinance in the South Pacific in World War II. He had been successful setting up a materials handling business in Nashville, Tennessee, but he had no retirement plan and was nearing that time of life when he would stop work and would need an income.

Would he lend me the money? It never hurts to ask.

My reasoning went this way: Capital is needed to grow. If I have to go to someone else to get it, who would I rather approach, a stranger or a family member? I had heard horror stories of money lent between family members—personal loans never paid back—and the resulting resentments and estrangements.

I had experience borrowing money from bankers. They had listened to each new story as I sold them on my ability to purchase and renovate a property. They had supported my budding career in real estate development. I knew I had the discipline to repay a loan, whether it was from a family member or anyone else. And besides, this plan had the added benefit that if the project was successful, it would provide my father a retirement income.

Meeting with my lawyer, we worked out a concept for a partnership agreement. The proposal to my father was that he put up $125,000 to purchase the three-acre parcel of land adjacent to the university. We would then each own half interest in the project—he would put up the cash, and I would build it. Working with my architect, we had determined forty apartments could be built on the site. The bank was willing to lend us all the money needed for construction, and they would consider the $125,000 purchase price for the land as our equity in the project. For his $125,000 investment, my father would receive all the tax write-off. I would receive all the cash flow, and in five years when he retired, we would share the cash flow equally.

It was an arm's-length transaction. I felt certain I had

the discipline to pay my father back so long as the project was successful. There was risk for us both, but he agreed. We formed Travis & Travis, a New York State Limited Partnership. I was general partner; my father was the limited partner. It was important to me that I be the one in control. Just in case push came to shove, I wanted to know where I stood. As long as I paid the debt on my father's money, I was the owner and in control of the company.

It served us well. I would honor my obligation to repay his loan at 8% interest as though it were an agreement with a stranger, but the terms were more lenient than I could ever have received from a stranger. It worked famously. Over the years we grew our holdings in Travis and Travis from one to many properties. My father retired comfortably on the income we received, and I had a source of capital. Rather than halving my income by forming a partnership, I had increased my ability to expand my real estate portfolio exponentially.

I had done a number of renovations but had never prepared a proposal for a project from the ground up. One weekend at his office, my architect gave me a crash course in ground-up real estate development. Over a Saturday and Sunday, we wrote a business plan for the bank. I knew the rental side of the business; he knew the construction side. I worked up the pro forma for operations once the project was built; he worked up the basic concept and layout for the building on the site, the costs of the foundations, the framing, the wiring, the plumbing—the thousands of details and decisions that go into putting up a new building. It was fascinating.

Within a week, the bank had approved the business plan and agreed to lend us $1.3 million. Within three weeks of visiting Mr. Yarnell, we had signed a purchase offer on the land with the university; we had developed the basic concept for the project; and we had secured a verbal commitment for the financing from the bank. I closed my film business and went to work full time as the general contractor building Ravenwood—a forty-unit apartment building across the street from the Cornell campus.

We bought an old house trailer for $500, moved it to the site for an office, and broke ground in October. My crews worked through the winter in temperatures as low as minus four degrees. We built 140-foot-long clear plastic tents over the foundations, in order to be able to heat the area with kerosene burners and pour concrete foundations through the winter. We sequenced the construction of four identical buildings. By the time the first one was half framed, the second one had the footer poured, the third one had the site cleared and the foundations dug, the final one was staked out ready to fit into the sequence when we got to it. We moved through the entire project in that manner. As the roof was going on the first building, the fourth building was being framed, and so on.

By March, we had rented the building entirely for August occupancy. We had 140 student tenants who were thrilled to be moving into new, high-quality accommodations with parking. We had rented 100% by advertising in the student newspaper. The newspaper had written a nice article when we broke ground for the project, and they kept up with the project on and off through the winter—news articles on your new project can be wonderful free advertising, and with the help of several ads and the articles in the student newspaper, all forty units rented based on what I came to call "a picture and a promise." We had the architect's pictorial rendering and the floor plans to show the students what the units would look like, and they had my promise it would be done in time for the fall semester.

We finished construction and furnished the units with new, quality furniture, and in mid-August, we held a party on-site for the workers, the city and university officials, the neighbors, and fellow landlords—celebrating the opening of Ravenwood, the first new apartment complex to be built near the university in probably forty years. I was feeling pretty proud of myself.

Through the construction process, I often marveled at the skill and perseverance of the fifty men working on the job at any one time. They were on the job by 7:30 a.m. every morning. They dug in the mud. They endured the frigid temperatures. They worked late when necessary to meet a deadline. They came in on weekends. They ran pipes and wires. They framed and roofed in below-zero temperatures. They installed windows. They finished the sheetrock walls and painted. Day after day they worked. I was motivated—creating an increment of a lifetime income—or falling on my face. But fear is a great motivator. I worked diligently keeping up with the subcontractors, ensuring that we stayed on schedule. I would ask the contractors for their bills and pay them before they had to even ask. My father and I had personally guaranteed the loan with the bank. I had little to lose through all this, but my father certainly did. To his credit, he maintained his equanimity throughout the project. We had much to gain. But the workers? What were they getting out of it?

This was by far the largest job I had ever tackled, requiring me to sign thousands of dollars of checks every week to pay each of the subcontractors. Certainly, they and their workers received a weekly paycheck, and that was their great motivator. But more than that going on. Why did men work like these guys did?

One Sunday, as I was on the job with the sheet rockers and the plumbers, who were working overtime to meet a deadline we simply could not miss, it came to me—these guys were working for a paycheck certainly, but they were also working for something else. They were working for the sheer satisfaction of a job well-done. It is brought up in us— do your job and do it right. They were there day after day, giving this project all they had, and they were doing it for the money, yes, but they were also doing it for the satisfaction of seeing a project take shape before their eyes and knowing they had taken part in it. These workers took pride in their craft, their skills, and the results. Realizing that, I renewed my attention and my praise to them daily, as they struggled through the winter's construction, for they were assisting me in creating an increment of a lifetime income.

CHAPTER 11

DESIRE'S AT THE HEART OF IT:
It Will Happen

Every limitation has its value,
but limitation that requires persistent effort
entails a cost of too much energy.

Jumping ahead to the mid-1990s, a Realtor friend of mine came to me with two properties: a fifty-one-unit apartment complex, and a twenty-unit apartment complex. They belonged to the estate of the late local cable company magnate, and his attorney had decided to sell them by sealed bid.

I took the Realtor to lunch. The attorney for the seller's estate was offering no commission on the deal. I could go directly to the attorney with my bid, but the Realtor was a friend, and we discussed how we might make this happen working together. He knew my preferred method of buying was with no money of my own in the deal. His sister had money to lend as she was recently widowed, and her husband—a very successful doctor, had left her quite well off. Her late husband had in fact invested with me in an earlier deal. The family trusted me.

During lunch, I offered to pay the Realtor $60,000 to make the deal happen. It was a number that simply came to me, as we sat together discussing how this might work for all parties. It was not a bribe. It was not illegal, it was simply a finder's fee—a sort of private commission, which should be enough to really motivate him to pull this deal together. If he would submit my bid, and if he would arrange for his sister to lend me enough money for the down payment on the purchase, he would earn $60,000. This amount was less than the 6% commission he would have made if he had a listing on the complexes, but the attorney was offering no commission, and $60,000 was certainly better than that. Another idea also came to me—would my friend finance his "commission" over a fifteen-year period at the current rate of interest? He saw the possibility for an ongoing monthly income, and he eagerly agreed. He would check with his sister to see if she would lend the $165,000 needed for me to purchase the properties.

Within hours he called me back, and we had a deal. We wrote up a purchase offer to submit to the attorney for the estate. Several days later, he came back to me and said it would be a good idea to increase the offer by about 10%. He knew the other people who were bidding, and the properties were still a good deal at the higher price, trusting his knowledge of the market and the competition in the bidding, I agreed.

Within a week, he told me I had been chosen as the successful bidder. Thanks to the effort of my Realtor friend and our creative financing package, I could now become the proud owner of seventy-one additional apartment units at no out-of-pocket expense, and these were apartments that needed no renovation, only proper management, for they were rented at rates that had not been raised in twelve years. There was a lot of potential for improving the income.

These properties were definitely a problem, but not ones that required dust and dirt to solve, only good financial management—they had been bought for no cash, only by asking for what I wanted and what seemed to make sense to all those involved. Granted, by then in my career, many years of experience negotiating deals had given me the ability to first, recognize a deal—an apartment complex where the rents have potential for increase to market. Second, to ask for what might seem like the moon, buying a $2 million property with no cash? And third, to know how to frame the transaction so that my friend got what he wanted—a commission, or finder's fee. His sister also got what she wanted, a significantly higher return on her cash than she could earn from CDs or the bank. Finally, I got what I wanted—two wonderful properties without having to sell others to raise the cash for the purchase, and this time it had all been done without getting my hands dirty!

As it has been with all my real estate deals, *desire was at the heart of this transaction*—the desire to create an independent income in real estate. Hold that desire yourself, and you will find that in your own way, in your own circumstances, the right deals will begin to present themselves to you.

By now, you have made your wish list. You know what it is you want. You have written your desires down—everything you want. And no one can take away your most private desires. They are yours. You know that in time they will be realized. Just hold them and read your list daily.

Something happens then. If you focus on what you really want and not on the fear of not getting it, not on your inability to speak, or your lack of experience, or your lack of money, but instead you focus on what you really want—gradually, you begin to get it. A simple desire will soon be checked off your list. Whatever it was has come to you—not through worrying about it, but just by having the desire and knowing what you want.

A sort of "click" will happen then, and you will realize that it is acceptable for you to have desires. You will realize that you can say what needs to be said at the right time. You will recognize the opportunities your desires are creating. With the desire as your focus, the fear of not getting it, of your inability, and of your inexperience disappear. You can recognize the steps, speak the right words and write the proposal. You will gain the skills to put yourself out there in whatever way it takes for you to make the deal—*to get what you want*. Not through sheer effort of will, but through a quiet confidence and trust that your desires are yours, that they are valid, and that you are entitled to see them realized for yourself—you will be able to get what you want.

Asking for what you want will become second nature, as will the skill of putting forward the proposal that results in your owning an income property at terms that work for you and for the seller. By repeating it over and over, until you find the right deal, the process will become more and more enjoyable.

Run the numbers. Ask the seller for the terms you need. Ask the bank for the terms you need. You know that eventually some combination of property, price, location, and terms will come together in a way that will enable you to own property. Don't worry about the exact way it will happen. It will happen. A deal will be made.

There are many different ways to get involved in real estate. It might be compared to, say, the grocery business. One can begin as a janitor or stock clerk, or one can become a manager. It is possible to own an entire grocery store or a chain of grocery stores locally or nationally. Or you can buy stock in a publicly traded chain of stores and become an investor.

In real estate, one can manage or work on houses for someone else and be paid a wage. Or simply purchase a property of your own, rent it, and become a manager. Once you've mastered that, perhaps purchase numerous multi-family buildings and manage them. Another possibility is to branch out into office and retail, warehouse, and specialty use buildings. You can stay local, or you can buy property anywhere in the country, or in the world. Or you can simply choose to buy stock in a publicly traded Real Estate Investment Trust (REIT) and become a silent partner or investor.

Just as with grocery stores, or any other area of business, there are many ways to invest in real estate. However you do it, just remember there is no inherent value in bricks and mortar. The only value a building has is in how it is used and what someone will pay for that use.

You may not be skilled with a hammer. If you are a professional in another field, the idea of handling the dirt and dust of a renovation and construction may not appeal to you as a way to buy a property with little or no money down. You may not have saved a significant sum for a down payment, but you still have the desire to own income property. Perhaps you have some money, but you don't know how to begin.

Look around you. Deals are made every day. Every day, people are getting what they want. Deals are made because each party to the deal feels it is in their best interest to agree to it. We tend to block ourselves by saying, "Oh, they will never agree to that," and we fail to ask, or we don't take the time to think through a possible solution based on what we want, and we walk away without ever having made the proposal for what we want. We don't feel confident enough to put forward our own thoughts and desires, and we fail to act. As a result, our situation doesn't change. We continue feeling suppressed and frustrated, for we know we could do more, be more, have more than we do, but we are afraid to act.

Larry, my brother-in-law in North Carolina, is an insurance broker. He has done well. In addition to selling insurance over the years, he and my sister Wendy have purchased seventeen income properties. Typically, they have purchased a property by finding a seller willing to hold a second mortgage and a banker willing to lend them the difference, or they have borrowed against equity built up in one property for the down payment on another. Typically, they put in no cash of their own. On the mantle in his office, he has a stack of bumper stickers collected over the years. The one on top reads "I started with nothing, and I still have most of it left." I can't help but smile at that, for that is how, for many years, I approached buying real estate. I began with nothing; if I lost it all, I would be no worse off than when I started!

It's amazing how quickly that attitude changes, however. With each property you purchase, you feel more secure, more independent from an employer, more able to set your own course. You learn to live with and accept a certain level of risk in exchange for an independent income from ownership of rental property.

CHAPTER 12

STEP BY STEP:
Several Examples of My Own Deals

When, however, the limitation is a natural one (as, for example, the limitation by which water flows only downhill), it necessarily leads to success, for then it means a saving of energy.

I often tell my bankers that I move forward step by step, completing one deal, assimilating it into my portfolio, and then going on to the next. Each deal is new in some way, and I take the next step by accepting it and taking it on. To me it seems a safe and methodical way to approach real estate acquisition. Speculation and get-rich-quick schemes are not part of my nature. The bankers seem to like my cautious approach.

Of course, you will find your own way of operating, but you might enjoy hearing how a couple of more deals came together for me—again with no out-of-pocket investment on my part: nothing more than the mounting desire to create an ever-expanding income in real estate.

Just as the construction of the forty-unit Ravenwood project was drawing to a close, a gentleman who owned a four-story building in Collegetown approached me. The building was over a century old and located a block from the main entrance to Cornell University at 407 College Avenue. He owned the building free and clear. He wanted to sell it and hold a mortgage and had offered it to my arch competitor, but he wanted to make sure it went into the best hands possible. He was also asking quite a high sum for the property and as any good businessman would do, he was checking around to see if he was getting the best deal. Of paramount importance, since he was going to offer to hold paper for the right buyer, he wanted to sell it to someone he could trust.

From the outside, the building resembled a four-story tenement with large porches across the front, and on the ground floor there were two retail stores, an electronics store and a record store. We climbed the stairs and walked through the building. It was a student rental. On each of the three upper floors, there were two "railroad apartments"—long, narrow units that require the resident to walk through one room to get to the next one in line—not very conducive to student living, or even comfortable family living. Interior stairs and a glass skylight and airshaft had been designed at the center of the building. There was no way the income from the poorly laid out units would justify the price he was asking for the building. To make it work, the building needed to be reconfigured, bedrooms needed to be added, and the wasted internal space for stairs and airshaft, somehow needed to be utilized.

We finished our tour of the building and stood outside in the walkway leading to the street. He asked me what I thought. I pulled a pen and a paper napkin from my pocket and thought for a moment. "Here is what I would do," I said, drawing an elongated rectangle on the napkin. "First, bisect the building the other way. Get rid of the long, narrow, railroad apartments. Construct two stair towers the height of the building midway along on each side. Instead of railroad apartments, divide it with a large eight-bedroom in the front half of the building and two three-bedrooms side by side in the back. That way, the central hallway and kitchens and baths can be integrated into useful space in the interior of the building. Building code does not require that kitchens and baths have direct light and ventilation, so we can maximize the number of bedrooms by placing them around the perimeter of the building with access to the windows. I know the eight-bedroom units will work in the student market."

He looked at my impromptu plan, thought for a moment, and then looked right at me. "This is fabulous! This will work," he said. "I will sell you the building." He spelled out the terms. He would hold the mortgage for 100% of the purchase price in second position, thereby enabling a bank to use the property as security for a first mortgage for construction. He would sell me the building for no cash down. He was agreeing to subordinate his mortgage for the purchase price to the construction loan from the bank, which would be needed to renovate the building into something that would produce significantly more income. My idea of utilizing the internal airshaft and stairwells would result in the ability to increase the rental rates and make enough money to pay his mortgage, pay the bank's mortgage, and be profitable for me.

We worked out the details in a written purchase offer with our attorneys. It was a formula similar to the one used on my two previous burned-out projects. With the seller's assistance, and the seller's trust, I became the owner of a building with thirty student tenants, and a plan for increasing it to over fifty. All of this, for no cash.

It was October. We closed on the property, and my dad

and I became the new owners. I had arranged the deal, but my father was my partner, and we went in together on this one, even though it required none of his cash. The student leases ran to May 30. We hired an architect, and together shepherded the renovation plan through the site-plan-review permitting process with the city.

During the spring, before we had even begun construction, students began renting apartments at 407 for the next school year, just as they had done at Ravenwood—on a "picture and a promise." The location was so desirable they couldn't wait to sign the leases, and although we always rent apartments on a twelve-month lease ("the bank wants their mortgage paid every month, and you are welcome to sublet," we tell them), for the first year, since we were going to open in August after the completion of construction, we offered ten-month leases that would begin the end of August when the students returned, and end the following June. The unbelievably convenient location a block from campus and the initial ten-month lease enabled us to rent 100% of the units, before we even began construction.

We had a rendering—a picture of the building, drawn to show what the building would look like when the work was completed. We turned the porches across the front into a modern façade with picture windows, and we added bedrooms. We had floor plans of the units. And I gave prospective tenants my word that the building would be ready in time for classes in the fall.

On May 30th, the current student tenants left for their summer break. On June 1st, we began what would become an eighty-seven-day renovation, gutting the entire building down to the bare studs, reconfiguring the units, constructing the two masonry stair towers, rewiring, re-plumbing, and finishing out eight new furnished apartments. We kept the stores open on the ground floor by building a scaffold with a covered walkway across the front of the building at sidewalk level to protect customers and passersby as they walked along the front of our construction site.

On August 27th, eighty-seven days after we had started, we held a party in the completed building for all the workers, the neighbors, fellow landlords, and the city officials. And as promised, the new residents moved in the next day in time for the fall semester. I had been at the job every morning at 7:30 a.m. all summer long. My crews had worked six days a week, and we had all worked around the clock the last couple of days before the opening. We had done it.

The early 1980s were a difficult time financially. I didn't follow the news much then, and it didn't seem to be affecting me personally, but the country was in a recession. After completing Ravenwood, there was adequate monthly income to support myself and meet the payments to my former wife and family, not regally, but sufficient to meet my ever-expanding obligations. I was focused simply on managing my existing projects and moving on to building the next one. By now there was a full-time person managing my office—my film studio was converted to a real estate management office—and I had one full-time maintenance worker.

The part of the recession that did affect me was interest rates. The prime rate of interest—the rate that major banks charge their best customers to borrow—climbed to 21%. Local banks were lending at 17%. The gentleman who sold me 407 College Avenue agreed to take back a second mortgage at 14%. It seemed like a real deal: 14% in second position on $525,000, with no cash in the deal, plus a bank loan for construction at 17%. The place had real potential, and even considering the high rate of interest, the income and expense numbers worked. As I saw it, I was putting in no cash, just a whole lot of sweat equity.

Projecting the rental income, once the renovation was complete we could increase the rent from $125 per month for each student to $225 per month—remember, this was 1982. I had a pretty good idea what the maintenance, management, taxes, and insurance would cost once the project was completed, and it had worked. The bank bought into it. I had the experience now.

I also had a significant mortgage from the seller at 14% for twenty-five years. He added one seemingly insignificant line to the deal, though: *"No prepayment."* I agreed to pay him $5,266 a month for twenty-five years, with no right to prepay the mortgage! He was not being greedy; it was a reflection of the market we were in at the time. He was giving me a good deal. However, ten, fifteen, twenty, twenty-two, twenty-three years later, when rates had come down to 12%, then 10%, 8%, then as far down as 6.5%, I was still paying the seller 14%. Over the years, we had become good friends. My wife and I visited him and his wife each winter in Florida. Whenever I brought up the idea of repaying his loan, he would smile and say a long drawn out, "Noooo…" He was very happy with his deal. I had signed it; I had agreed to the deal; I would honor it.

It got to be almost a joke between us. Each year as the

end of the loan term came closer, I would ask to prepay him, and each year he would say "Noooo…"—he was very happy with his deal, and deep down, I had no regrets either. The property had tripled in value over the years. Rents had gone from $225 per student to over $600 per student. I was paying 14% interest, but those terms had allowed me to purchase an asset that was worth it, with no cash of my own—only an idea of how to take a basically worthless shell and turn it into a producing property. My last payment was made in 2007. We are still good friends. I kept my word. He kept his. Neither of us have any regrets.

I would recommend to you, however, that when you negotiate loans from individuals, *always* try to negotiate the right to prepay them.

CHAPTER 13

A GIANT STEP:
Business Is Human Interaction

---

*The energy, that otherwise would be consumed
in a vain struggle with the object, is applied wholly to the
benefit of the matter at hand, and success is assured.*

Halfway through the 407 College Avenue renovation in the summer of 1982, my architect for the Ravenwood project came to me and said the City of Ithaca was preparing a Request for Proposals (RFP) to select a developer to "spearhead the renovation of Collegetown." He asked if I would be interested in joining him. Two years earlier, we had spent a long weekend together working up the Ravenwood concept and business plan. It had been tremendously successful; 407 College Avenue had also been successful. It was time to move forward, and here was the opportunity. We spent several days developing a plan and writing a response to the RFP.

As full of myself as I was from my recent successes, it was totally evident to me that my real strength lay in assembling the right team—the best architect, the best accountant, and the best attorney in town joined our ranks. Although he had already invested most of his ready cash in building Ravenwood, my father fully supported the project in concept. We were also partners in the 407 property and were both enjoying the benefits of these projects. I felt confident that somehow, we could raise the money for this multimillion-dollar plan that was evolving.

On the day of the presentations to the city and university officials, out of three respondents to the RFP, we were the last to present. The first presentation was by a group comprised of the largest construction contractor in town, who did $40 million a year in construction, the owner of the largest car dealership in town, and several investors. They presented a plan for an $8 million hotel on the city parking lot adjacent to the university. They obviously had the firepower to make the project happen.

The next group to present was Turner Construction, from New York City, one of the largest real estate developers in the country. They showed an elaborate presentation of the projects they had completed over the past sixty or seventy years—including the Flat Iron Building in New York City, the United Nations building, the US Supreme Court building, and a host of others.

I was ready to crawl under my chair. Their proposal was to build a large underground parking garage with an open pedestrian plaza on the top. In addition, they proposed a hotel, retail shops, apartments, and student condominiums. Their elaborate plans for the project depicted total redevelopment of the entire four-block area and would cost $25 million. We had definitely been outgunned.

A quizzical expression formed on the face of the Cornell vice president as the Turner representative explained their proposal to use Cornell's credit to build the project. They would sell the project upon completion, repay Cornell with a healthy return, and then leave town. It was obvious that as elaborate as the Turner plan was, they had laid no ground-work with the university. The Cornell VP was hearing of it for the first time. "Use Cornell's credit?" That was a novel idea …

As novel as it was, everyone could see it gained no trac-tion with the university vice president that day. We made our own simple presentation for two towers with about forty student apartments each to be built on the hillside that was the city parking lot. My team presented well, but we, and certainly I, had the resources of a pauper compared to these two experienced companies. My team left the meeting that afternoon feeling more than a little depressed.

A week later, the city planner called me to set up a meet-ing at city hall. I sat with him and listened as he told me our group had been selected by the city and the university to be the "Preferred Developer for Collegetown." I couldn't have been more surprised. We had won!

The city planner told me that the selection panel thought our idea was the best one for the site. The construction group could certainly have pulled it off, but in the selection panel's opinion, a hotel was not the best use of the site. In addition, the Turner group's proposal had totally surprised the vice president of Cornell. They were not about to let Turner use the university's credit to raise $25 million. Besides, their proj-ect was totally unrealistic. There were thirty or forty different property owners who would have to agree to be bought out in order to build the garage, the pavilion, and all that they pro-posed. Turner was a big-city developer and not at all sensitive to Ithaca. He said they felt our project was of an appropriate scale and that student housing was the best use for the site. Our track record with Ravenwood and 407 College Avenue was modest but solid, and they had chosen us.

This was a giant step for me. After ten years of "playing the game," my real estate holdings were around $3 million. This project would give me the opportunity to double or triple my holdings. Based on my experience with both the Ravenwood and 407 College Avenue, we would have the Collegetown project designed and built within a year! It was the summer of 1982, and my modest independent income in real estate had long since been established, but my desires had increased. I was hooked, and ready to keep going.

Mr. Petrillose, who had sold me the burned-out Eddy Street house, owned a small parcel of land that had been a service station for fifty years and was surrounded on three sides by the parking lot which the city had designated as the core site for the Collegetown redevelopment. I went to see him. He told me it had been his dream since the 1940s to acquire that parking lot and develop it, together with his parcel, into a large housing complex for students. He had preliminary plans drawn up in the 1940s, but neither the city nor the university had been interested. He was delighted to assist me. He agreed to give me an option on his parcel for $1,500. As preferred developer, I now had the right to negotiate with the city and the university to purchase their land for the project, but a central piece that would be necessary for our project, or any project to be built, was now under my control.

Our one-year project stretched into two, then three, then four years, and each year Mr. Petrillose renewed the option at no additional charge. He liked me, he trusted me, and based on my success renovating his burned-out Eddy Street building, he had the confidence that I could bring the project in. Struggling through the design of four different plans over as many years, and the city vacillating on their involvement in the project, and as other developers attacked me and demanded their turn to try to develop the site, it was Mr. Petrillose and the option on the service station parcel that kept me in control of the site.

It was from that experience that I realized the first rule of real estate development: *Site Control.* There is no use wasting your time and money on dreams and designs unless you control the site. It had been the case in building Ravenwood, when my father and I bought the land from Cornell University. It had been the case in the rebuilding of 407 College Avenue. It will be the case with every real estate project you undertake—every successful project begins with site control!

The university had signed a purchase offer with me for the Ravenwood site, which allowed me to move ahead with design and financing and construction. It was the same now. I controlled a key piece of the Collegetown site, the most desired real estate in Ithaca, with only a $1,500 option—and I had the option because an elderly gentleman took a liking to me, and I was helping fulfill his forty-year-old dream.

As you buy your first property, and your second and beyond, and as you continue toward your goal of creating an independent income in real estate, you will probably find, as I did, that each project tends to take on a life of its own. I used to think that business was just business—cold, impersonal, nothing more than numbers. But business is much more than that. Business is human interaction. As you move through your transactions step by step, you may meet brick walls along the way. Flail away at them, and they often crumble brick by brick, or you may find a way to go around them. If they do not crumble, you can turn and go in a different direction altogether. Continue on this path, and solutions will often come from the people around you—from the word said that sparks an idea, from the support of a mentor, or from a friend who comes at just the right time to bolster your courage or bring you a solution. You will interact and make deals with borrowers, with sellers, with bankers and with tenants. It's fascinating. It's people. It's you at your best. I have found business to be one of the epitomes of human interaction.

As you borrow money, it would be good to realize you are dealing with other people's livelihood and dreams. Imagine yourself someday lending money, holding a mortgage, or selling a property and holding paper, or even owning a bank and lending money. Your financial well-being will become dependent on the person who has agreed to pay you back. If they leave, if they walk out, or if for whatever reason they cannot or will not honor their obligation to repay you, you will suffer the financial deprivation and loss.

Business is human interaction. Words and money are part of the energy that flows between us. It is a fascinating, satisfying, and extremely creative process. It takes courage to begin the trip, to take the first step, to put yourself out there day after day in the process of doing business. But if you choose to do that—to borrow money and buy a property—and if you stay involved in the flow and in the process, great wealth and happiness can come to you. If you choose not to get involved, to stay indoors, out of the fray, playing video games and watching TV—you will have a different life. Only you can know which is the right course for you to follow.

CHAPTER 14

BRICK WALLS CRUMBLE:
We Stuck with the Process

---

*The limitation must
be carried out in the right way
if it is to be effective.*

We had won the competition to become the preferred developer for Collegetown, and we dubbed our new project "Eddygate" in honor of the lovely two-story Victorian stone gate adjacent to the property and which used to be the main entrance to Cornell University.

In my inexperience and enthusiasm, I had thought the project would take no longer than a year to develop. I was wrong. It took four years and as many designs to even begin construction, and while the architect had done the initial design work for us on spec, to develop each design to the level the city would need for approval would cost us close to $100,000. I did not have that kind of money to put down on speculative design. Neither did my father, since he had essentially invested his life's savings in Ravenwood. We stuck with the process, however. Our giant step was moving forward by baby steps, but it was still moving forward.

One day, out of the blue, my Realtor friend called me and told me of a 110-unit apartment complex named Sweden Hills located about two hours away near SUNY Brockport.

The seller wanted $1.9 million for it. My friend told me a little bit about the project. He showed me the pro forma—the income and expenses for the property—and we decided to drive the two and a half hours to Brockport, New York, to check it out. When we arrived and drove down the long driveway, past the pond, past a dozen cedar-sided, hip-roofed buildings, each one with a balcony, I was swept away, and on impulse told him I would buy it.

I had no money for the down payment but had read about syndications. Surely there should be a way to make this deal work. It was an attractive, well-cared-for complex, and a first look the numbers showed that it worked financially. We toured the project. Sitting in the management office with the on-site manager we reran the numbers. It became more and more evident that it should be possible to raise the money for the purchase from investors, own a portion of the project, and walk away from the closing with money in our pockets.

Over the next couple of weeks, we negotiated the deal down to $1.65 million. Nine 10% limited-partnership interests were sold to friends, and to clients of my accountant at $50,000 each. With the cash flow the project would generate, coupled with the accelerated depreciation that was available prior to the 1986 change in the Income Tax Law, each investor would realize well over a 10% annual return. My father and I would retain a 10% ownership position, and I would manage the project for a management fee of 6.5% of gross income.

It wasn't planned this way, and it wasn't readily apparent how things would turn out. It was an impulse, when driving down the driveway I told the Realtor that we would buy it, but as it unfolded, the entire project took on a life of its own. We prepared a non-registered offering plan, since it was a small enough deal not to require registration with, and approval of the Securities and Exchange Commission. With contacts from my accountant and a few friends, we sold the partnership interests within a couple of weeks. We closed on the property, and after paying $200,000 for the down payment and closing costs we walked away with $250,000 in our pockets.

It had been a roundabout path. We had sold another $150,000 in limited partnership interests in the 407 College Avenue property, and now had enough money for the Eddygate design and development. We had followed our noses you might say, followed an opportunity that had come our way, and in doing so, had raised the development capital to build the new project.

Along with the award as preferred developer for College-town, the city was offering a Department of Housing and Urban Development (HUD) loan at 1% interest in the form of a second mortgage; the amount of the HUD loan would be based on the number of jobs created by the project. We quickly scrapped the two-tower design for Eddygate. More jobs would be created from the operation and management of a hotel than a housing complex. Our architect drew up a plan for a hotel on the site—we had the design completed and a rendering drawn for an eight-story hotel in the heart of Collegetown. We then hired a New York City firm to conduct a feasibility study for a hotel. They did their research and found they could project neither the room rate nor the occupancy rate as being adequate to make the hotel feasible. Our dreams were momentarily shattered.

The city was planning a parking garage as part of the overall development. Since a hotel was not feasible, perhaps we could build apartments less expensively on air rights above a city parking structure. Our architect designed a project above the proposed city garage that would look out over the town. Everyone liked the project design and the city proceeded with working drawings on their parking structure. We paid our architect to draw up schematic-level drawings for the apartments. The city put their project out to bid, but their lowest bid came back at $1.2 million over their budget. This entire process had taken the better part of a year, but at the next council meeting the city voted to scrap the project.

Even as the "preferred developers" for Collegetown we were now left without a building site. I stewed for a few days and then went to City Hall to see the City Planner. The only way I would continue, I said, was if the city would sell us the strip of land along the street. That way we would control our own destiny. The city could build their parking garage on the interior of the site or not, but we would be able to continue without them if necessary. *Site control*—we needed that, in- dependent of the city, if we were going to continue spending money for design and development. My architect drew up a few sketches for a project along the street, which we pre- sented to city council, and at their next meeting they agreed to the change in the project. By this point, however, other developers were clamoring for their turn at the site. My team had been working on it for three years, and we had yet to see anything tangible. I still held the option on the Petrillose parcel, and while the city could have taken it from me by eminent domain, they were reluctant to appropriate private land for another developer's use, so I felt relatively safe. In any case, the city reaffirmed our team as preferred developer and agreed to sell us the strip of land along the street.

My architect redesigned the site plan to include an eight-story apartment building on the new site along the street. The city approved the new design and redid its own plans for a free-standing garage on the interior of the block behind our proposed building along the street front. By then HUD had a different program—one tied to affordable housing rather than job creation. We were able to finance the project with tax-exempt bonds and the government HUD loan, in exchange for making 20% (thirteen of sixty-four) of the apartment units available for low income tenants. This was not difficult, however, since many of the graduate students at Cornell were earning incomes well below the maximum set by HUD. We would be able to keep our student mix and also meet HUD requirements. In August of 1986, we broke ground on the $5.2 million project. It opened in August of 1987, again fully rented from a "picture and a promise." I was humbled by the length and complexity of the development process. No longer did I feel like a hotshot developer who could build a complex project in a year or less.

Eddygate had taken a long time. In my enthusiasm, I had originally projected we would have it designed, financed and constructed within a year. It had taken five years from our selection as preferred developer until our ribbon cutting. But Eddygate was a grand building and a true exercise in public/ private partnership. The city and Cornell had the original vision for attracting a developer to put in the first "window box" in Collegetown, so to speak. Since then, Cornell had renovated two major dormitories adjacent to our site and had spent $26 million on a new performing arts center. The city had built a new parking garage behind Eddygate, and it had also been the conduit for what became the low-interest Urban Development Action Grant loan that enabled us to build the project. During a single year, $40 million of construction had gone up on this one block in Collegetown, beginning with our initial development.

Our building was only a small part of the reconstruction of Collegetown. At eight stories, Eddygate was impressive—the building structure followed the curve of the street as it wound down the hill from College Avenue. It housed sixty-four student apartments with over 180 students, and seven retail stores on the ground floor. The total project cost was $5.2 million—a small fortune for me at the time.

While I was engaged in the initial development for Eddygate and the innumerable negotiations required to bring any project to completion, we had purchased a number of other properties—Sweden Hills, with 110 units—the sale of the limited partnership interests for it had generated $250,000, which together with the money from the sale of the 407 College Avenue limited partnerships, had enabled us pay for the Eddygate design and development.

We had also purchased Lakeland, a thirty-two-unit apartment complex adjacent to the university. For this we offered a limited partnership interest to two of the original partners in Sweden Hills, who had also later bought into 407 College Avenue, after the project had been completed and the risks associated with construction and overruns were past.

My uncle, who was a Realtor, brought me the Westview project, a brick complex with several buildings, totaling fifty-six units—again adjacent to the university. I offered that to my partners as well, but they declined, so my father and I then refinanced Ravenwood, raising the needed $165,000 for the down payment on Westview, and bought it ourselves. By the mid-1980s we had bootstrapped our total portfolio from the single-family house purchased in 1973 by taking over the payments, to a total of 300 units. We didn't own them all outright, but we controlled that many units in our portfolio, and we controlled the management.

It was important to me to retain control over any project with partners—hence the limited partnership interests we offered. A limited partner puts up money to buy into a project. They receive a percentage of the cash flow based on the percentage of their interest, and they receive a percentage of the gains or losses. There can be considerable tax advantage for a limited partner—not only do they receive cash, provided the project is successful, but the savings on their taxes from the depreciation can boost their overall return significantly. They invest, but they have no "say-so" in the management decisions regarding a project. One gets their money, but without their input or direction. They are "silent partners." In exchange they have no risk beyond their original investment.

If a partner puts up $50,000 for a 10% interest, and the project throws off $100,000 in cash flow, the limited partner will have received $10,000 on their investment, or 20% cash-on-cash return. If the project loses money, it is the responsibility of the general partner, me, to come up with the cash needed. The investors have no responsibility to put in more money. This is a great incentive for the general partner to manage the properties in a manner that makes money. It was nice to get the investor's cash, as it enabled us to buy and control properties we would not otherwise have been able to afford at that stage of our development.

The typical scenario had us putting in no money. The partners would put up the cash required for the down payment on the purchase of a property, and we would own a percentage of the deal in exchange for our having assembled the project. At 407 we retained 70% ownership. At Lakeland, we owned 33%. We owned Westview, which we had purchased for slightly under $2,000,000, outright, and we were able to do this by refinancing the forty units at Ravenwood to raise the money for the down payment. This was no different than borrowing $5,000 against the equity in my first house to purchase the next house, only now there were simply additional zeros added to the number.

Site control had been my first rule of development. *Ownership control* became my first rule in partnerships. It was amazing to me how many people now approached me to ask about buying in as partners in our real estate deals. Once you have the experience purchasing and managing your first few properties, if you choose to grow more quickly than you might by following the 2-4-8-16 formula, partnerships may be the way to go. You can control and manage a larger portfolio of properties than you might be able to assemble alone, and you can own a significant percentage of each deal and retain ownership control as the general partner.

Here were the steps: *Find the deal. Structure the deal,* and it was here that I leaned heavily on my accountant to give me the parameters an investor might expect in an investment package. *Close the deal.* It was a quick, safe way to expand. It was this formula we used in the construction of Eddygate. My father and I put in the money we had made from selling the limited-partnership interests in Sweden Hills and 407 College Avenue as seed money to design and develop the project. We had site control, in that our team had been named preferred developer and we had the option on the Petrillose lot at the center of the site—which enabled us to negotiate with the city and Cornell to create the best possible project on the site. But it would take another $600,000 cash to begin construction. Ravenwood had been in operation for nearly five years, and the rents (and hence the value) had probably increased enough to support an appraisal that would allow the bank to extend that amount of cash to us on a second mortgage. However, we didn't want to strain our portfolio with too much debt. We had borrowed prudently. We owned properties that were all producing positive cash flow. We really wanted to build Eddygate, but we needed more cash.

I approached two of the partners who had joined me in 407 College Avenue and Sweden Hills and offered them the opportunity to buy into the deal. After lengthy discussion, they each agreed to put up $300,000. It would be a loan to the project. They would receive 8% simple interest on their money, and we would pay it back out of the cash flow as cash allowed. I projected it would take ten years to pay them off. Not only would they receive 8% on their money, but they also would each own 37.5% of the building, or a total of 75%. My family, who was now guaranteeing construction costs and any overruns on the project, would own 25%. Once the partners were paid off, their percentage ownership would drop to 25% each, and my family would own 50%. It was a stiff deal, but it would give us the cash we needed and essentially reward us with significant ownership for having structured the deal and built the building—they would be limited partners and I would be the general partner responsible for all aspects of financing, construction, and management.

It had worked. Human interaction is at the heart of business. The project had taken on a life of its own. And no matter how difficult things seemed at times, we were able to follow the process and make it happen.

This hard-core business transaction had involved literally hundreds of people, from City and Cornell officials who had the original dream of renovating Collegetown, to the designers, bond holders, suppliers, contractors, and material manufacturers—hundreds of people had contributed to the end product. Together we had delivered a high-quality building that would lead the way in changing the face of housing in the college community.

No longer could absentee landlords get by with giving students run-down junk to live in. They could simply no longer compete. Over the next few years, new projects began springing up, and as the city and Cornell officials had predicted, the entire student housing stock began to be upgraded. The brick walls we had had to confront all through the development process had somehow crumbled one by one, brick by brick. The cash had appeared, as we needed it. By sticking with the process, by having the Desire, the Drive, and the Discipline to persevere, my team and I had Delivered the project.

Our opening party was huge. Cornell officials, city officials, neighbors, the entire workforce that had built the building, friends, family, and even some of the future tenants attended. By now, it was a well-ensconced tradition in our company that whenever we opened a project, whether new or renovated, we celebrated with the workers, the bankers, and the community. We had coffee mugs and beer steins made with a red outline of the eight-story building on one side, and "I built Eddygate!" on the other. We gave them out in sets to the workers and guests at our party. "I built Eddygate!" Each worker, each banker, each city and Cornell official could celebrate with us. We had truly done it together.

CHAPTER 15

WELLSLEY AND MATT'S SUCCESS:
Be All You Can Be

---

*If we impose restrictions on others only,
while evading them ourselves, these restrictions will
always be resented and will provoke resistance.*

Burlington, North Carolina, is a sleepy little town close to the Chapel Hill/Raleigh/Durham Research Triangle, and a half hour drive east of Greensboro. The textile mills have closed, and the business has moved to China. Amtrak whizzes through the heart of the downtown three or four times a day, and although the train still stops upon occasion, the railroad depot is now a museum. LabCorp, a pharmaceutical research and manufacturing company, has bought a large portion of Downtown Burlington. They employ a workforce of over 3,500. It is LabCorp and, as my son-in-law Mike calls it, "society living on itself," that seems to keep the town going.

It was in Burlington that Wellsley, my niece, and her husband, Matt, chose to settle. They were in their late twenties. Wellsley had been a swimmer at North Carolina State, and prior to that, since age five, she had been a gymnast until injuries finally pulled her to the sidelines. Her discipline, determination, and sheer grit approached those of a soldier in the US Army: "Be All You Can Be!"

Wellsley had planned to go to medical school, but the

MCATs has gotten the best of her—three times, and she decided to join her future husband and become an EMT. Matt's grandfather had created the Raggedy Ann and Andy series of books for children in the 1930s. His grandmother had brought him up in Chapel Hill, and when he and Wellsley married, she had given them her house there in exchange for a small apartment in it, and their agreeing to care for her as she aged. It was a comfortable arrangement for both parties. She had since died, and they had sold her house and were now looking for a real estate project to sustain them.

They had watched me over the years. Wellsley's parents, my sister and her husband, had purchased seventeen houses in nearby Greensboro while she was growing up. Wellsley had observed the power of credit and the possibilities it offered for creating an independent income in real estate. Through her parents, for most of her life she had been exposed to the annual cycle of renting apartments, maintaining apartments, and turning them over each year to new tenants.

Wellsley and Matt called me one day. They had found a vacant furniture factory for sale in nearby Mebane, North Carolina. The factory was 275,000 square feet—nearly as long as a football field—and it was in the heart of downtown Mebane, an even sleepier little town than Burlington. They asked if I would come down and talk them through the development process. They envisioned turning the building into a complex of housing, shops, restaurants, and theatres. They said they had no money and wanted to get my advice on how to proceed. I shuddered a bit at the magnitude of their vision for a first project but said of course I would come. My son, Frost agreed to join us; he had completed his master's degree in Real Estate Development at Cornell and was working for a very successful real estate developer based in New Jersey. Together we would come for a weekend and assist Wellsley and Matt in analyzing (and probably trying to talk them out of) their dream project.

The White Furniture Factory in downtown Mebane seemed a dream come true for someone with lots of money to sink in a century-old structure, thirty minutes from one of the country's major markets. The town of Mebane was un-discovered—a railroad track paralleled the dusty main street through the heart of town. A few shops and feed stores lined the central two or three blocks comprising the downtown. Raleigh, Chapel Hill, and Durham all lay within a half hour's drive. Wellsley and Matt toured us through the giant, anti-quated brick structure with maple floors stained from a cen-tury of paint, lacquer, and machine oil from the lathes, saws, and paint booths used in the manufacturing process. The win-dows were steel frame and the post-and-beam structure was exposed throughout. The floors were at varying levels, and one could see the additions to the building that had been con-structed as the company expanded over the years. It was easy to imagine the shops and apartments, the restaurants and ca-fes that would someday fill this potential indoor atrium mall.

Frost and I listened while Wellsley and Matt explained their vision for the building—where the apartments would go, the stores, the open spaces, and the restaurants. By this time in my career, I had salvaged and renovated a dozen or more buildings ranging from single-family houses to a 50,000-square-foot, six- story warehouse in Ithaca, but for a first project, this one seemed simply daunting.

After hearing their plan, we began backing into the numbers. The project was a total of 275,000 square feet. Based on my recent experience renovating a warehouse project in Ithaca into an office building, we calculated it would cost approximately $85 per square foot to renovate the White Furniture Factory. At $85/sq. ft., we showed them, the total project cost would be just over $23 million. We stood in the dim light on the factory floor amidst the smells and old machinery. I ran the numbers on my pocket calculator, and Wellsley and Matt listened while we explained that typically for a project of that magnitude, a bank would require something in the order of 25% of the project cost, or $5.8 million. We asked them if they had thought about how they might raise that amount.

They said they had not thought seriously about it but added that they had listened to my stories of following one's desires. They had observed my success in developing projects with no money down, or with all borrowed money. They knew that I had always promoted the idea that you can do anything you want to do, and they thought they could sort of dream this project into existence.

Their comment gave me pause, for it is one thing to dream and desire, but it is important as well, while keeping the dreams and desires in one's heart and mind, to stay grounded in reality, to start from where one is in life, and to operate within the boundaries of one's limits and abilities. I suggested to them that to begin with a project of this size for their first one was a little more than what I had in mind when I had said you can do anything you want to. Maybe initially they should scale back and consider something more manageable in size. This town had yet to be discovered. They would be pioneers, with all the risk that might entail—they would need deep pockets to survive while they worked on this project and waited for the market to catch up.

I felt badly puncturing their enthusiasm but didn't want to be responsible for catapulting them into immediate bankruptcy—not that any bank would touch this project without a sophisticated, well-heeled investor behind it. I envisioned their spending two or three years thinking, planning, raising money possibly, and struggling to make ends meet in the meantime.

Frost and I suggested that if they liked this town, and it did have great potential being so close to the North Carolina Research Triangle and still undiscovered—we should look around and see if we could possibly find a property that would produce immediate income for them, since that is what they really needed.

It didn't take long to drive around downtown Mebane. We found one fairly new, two-story apartment project with pale yellow aluminum siding. We estimated from a count of the electric meters on the back corner of the building that it was probably twenty units. We told them this sort of project might work for them, depending on whether it was for sale, and if the seller was willing to hold secondary financing. The problem here was that it was newly constructed. The asking price, if it even were for sale, would probably be too high for them to put the financing together and still have a positive cash flow. The problem with this property from just the drive-by was that there was no problem, at least not one that was immediately apparent. There would be no immediate upside to be realized from solving anything, and they would probably pay top dollar, if it were for sale.

Wellsley and Matt were still smarting from the disappointment they felt at our quick financial analysis and depiction of the reality of tackling the White Furniture Company as their first project. They suggested that they take us into Durham to show us the old tobacco warehouse district. They explained that it was the renovation of the tobacco warehouses that had inspired them to think about the furniture factory as a possibility in the first place. Frost and I agreed, and we set out for Durham.

An incredible vision had been at work in Durham. Developers had reclaimed hundreds of thousands of square feet of derelict tobacco warehouses in the heart of the city and turned them into productive offices, shops, apartments, and community space. A small stream and waterfall cascaded down the central garden between long rows of soft red brick buildings that had been transformed into a thriving community in downtown Durham. We could see the appeal these had and why Wellsley and Matt were inspired to tackle the Mebane project.

By now it was late in the day, and we drove with them to my sister's house in Greensboro. That evening we took everyone to dinner. In an attempt to salvage the trip and put a positive spin on it all, Frost offered to work with them after dinner building an Excel spreadsheet and analyzing what we had seen that day, what it would take to renovate the White Furniture Company building, and what an operating statement for it would look like. At least they would have a prototype they could use, once they found a project more appropriate for a beginning—maybe a five or ten-unit building would be better for a start. Their desire was really to create an independent income in real estate. How they went about it was the key. They had identified their core desire, and we reassured them that things would eventually fall in line, even though they may at first seem not to.

Frost returned to New Jersey, and I returned to Ithaca. One could only admire the enthusiasm and courage of my niece and her husband. I still felt badly having punctured their White Furniture balloon, but it had seemed the right thing to do.

Several weeks later, I received an enthusiastic call from Wellsley. They had found a project in Burlington, only ten minutes' drive from Mebane, and even closer to their home in Chapel Hill. The building was twenty units with potential to be twenty-one, and just a block from the center of downtown Burlington. Burlington was bigger by far than Mebane, and much closer to Chapel Hill. She and Matt thought the area would appeal to the huge Chapel Hill market within a half hour's drive, if not just to the local Burlington people. It was built in 1928. It was two-story brick, with steel-frame windows, which was not a plus, but it had hardwood floors and nice-sized units. It was called Courtyard Apartments.

Wellsley explained that what had gotten them so excited about it was that the owners really wanted to sell. They had bought it last year out of foreclosure. The bank had recently foreclosed on the property for $800,000. Prior to that, a young couple had bought the property from the original owner for $400,000. They had sold the bank on their plan for a complete renovation. The bank lent them all the money for the renovation—$400,000, up front, and for some strange reason the couple prepaid their contractor. The contractor took the $400,000 and, without doing a lick of work, left for the Caribbean. The couple ended up in divorce; they couldn't do the construction without their contractor and their money. The bank had foreclosed for the $800,000 they owed, they lost the property, and these two new guys had bought it. I commented that it seemed like an exercise in stupidity—inexperience and stupidity.

Wellsley went on to say that the new buyer had picked up the foreclosed property for $450,000 from the bank. They had put in new HVAC and electrical service. They began repairing the units, but the falling plaster, the leaking windows, and dozens of holes in the walls had finally gotten the best of them. The time and work to bring the property back was more than they could handle, and they just wanted out.

She described the tenants as less than desirable. The rents were approximately $250 a month for a two-bedroom apartment and the property was run-down. In fact, she said, it was truly a wreck of a place. The leases were month-to-month, and there was a large vacancy—probably a third of the units were unoccupied.

As she ran through all the problems, my thought was of the opportunities this property might present. This might be the one. She and Matt also saw the problems as opportunities—how much did the sellers want for it? They wanted $650,000. They owed $450,000 and would settle for $500,000. Wellsley explained that they had agreed to take back a second mortgage for the $50,000, and subordinate to the bank's first mortgage for the purchase and renovation.

This sounded ideal: they had a seller who was really discouraged and wanted to sell. Wellesley said he simply was sick of it and didn't want to manage it anymore. He had given up.

They both felt that it would be a perfect renovation project. She and Matt had checked the local rental market and figured out that if they spent $20,000 a unit renovating the building, they would be able to get $650 a month rent for each apartment. They had already looked at the layout, and Matt had drawn a plan for combining a number of the units and enlarging them. The floors were oak, and they planned to refinish them. They had an engineer look at the building, and it was a solid structure. The previous owners had updated the electrical service. The roof seemed fine. They would put in new kitchens and baths. The boiler could be replaced, but basically it was a sound building that had been let go. They had run the numbers, and if they could get the financing, do the renovation, and rent it, they would make between $20,000 and $25,000 a year clear.

What would they do about the existing tenants? Their plan was to begin renovating the vacant units. They would do one unit at a time. They would then give the current tenants the choice of moving into a renovated unit at the new rent or moving out. The tenants were on month-to-month leases, so technically Wellsley and Matt could empty out the building in thirty days, but they were choosing to work with the tenants. They felt that most of them would probably move on, since they didn't seem the type of tenant who would want to pay the market rate for a newly renovated apartment.

Did they have a bank lined up? They were working on it and had talked to several local banks. One of them appeared really interested, and they felt fairly certain they would lend them the amount of the construction costs based on the renovated value. The bank wanted to see a business plan before they would commit—a normal request.

This sounded perfect. The bank came back with an offer: they would agree to the $50,000 second mortgage from the seller. Wellsley and Matt would put down $80,000, and the bank would finance the rest. With this they could control a project that would cost approximately $900,000 to purchase and renovate and be worth something over $1,000,000 when it was done.

That was exactly what they were thinking. They thought the property could then create almost enough income for them to live on and allow them give up their EMT jobs.

Who would do the work on the building? They both agreed that Matt could run the construction job. He had rebuilt his grandmother's house and created an apartment for her. He knew enough about construction to renovate a unit at a time. He would hire help with the electrical and plumbing, and probably a laborer to assist, but he could basically manage the entire job. Wellsley would do the bookkeeping and the renting.

As for the $80,000 to put down on the project, they said they had saved about $5,000 and wondered if I might consider lending them the rest. They would pay me back once the project was completed and they had refinanced the construction loan into a permanent loan with their bank.

I liked Wellsley's direct manner and her obvious competence. I told them it was a possibility, but first they should prepare a business plan that showed their projections for construction, and an operating statement projecting income and expenses once the project was completed. With those in place, I would consider it.

How had they found this place? Wellsley said they had found it through the Multiple Listing Service (MLS). After the White Furniture project and the taste of reality Frost and I had given them, they had begun looking on the Internet. They were willing to relocate. They were looking for anything four units and up and had looked all the way from Virginia to South Carolina.

The primary things they were looking for were location, potential for growth, profit, and owner financing. They wanted a project that would generate cash flow right away. They wanted to be in a good location. Plus, they wanted a project that had an upside, one with low rents that could be increased to market, and they wanted to buy it with enough owner financing to cover the down payment. She and Matt had thought long and hard and developed a detailed list of what they would need to succeed.

Wellsley said that that combination had not been easy to find. All the places they had looked at were either in a poor location with nothing around and no growth potential, or like Charlotte: developers had already found it, and the prices were too high to allow for much upside potential. And forget owner financing. Everything that seemed to be available had already been renovated or was new, and the sellers were after the highest price and all their cash. She said they had looked at literally dozens of places in three states and had actually made offers on seven different projects.

They had found seven projects and made seven offers. Their perseverance impressed me. But then Matt told me that every one of the owners had turned them down when they got to the owner financing part. Finally, they had gotten lucky.

They had found Courtyard Apartments through the MLS. It was located in Burlington, which was twenty minutes from where they lived in Chapel Hill. They had driven over and found Burlington to be relatively undiscovered. New development had passed it by. It was well situated near the Research Triangle, but it was run-down. The Courtyard Apartments were located two blocks from the center of town. They had called the Realtor and found the owner was asking $650,000 for twenty units but would settle for $500,000. The basement could be converted to an additional one-bedroom unit. It would then have two studios, eight two-bedrooms, and eleven one-bedroom apartments. The Realtor had taken them through the building. It was a wreck. Every apartment was rented month to month. It was full of problems, but Wellsley said all they could see was the potential.

I was truly impressed. Their enthusiasm and far-reaching aspiration for the White Furniture Company had been channeled into finding a project in an even stronger location, one that could be purchased at a severely discounted price due to the problems the seller was having with it. Once renovated, it could produce an income for Wellsley and Matt far beyond that of a five or ten-unit building. They were launched. If they were able to get their offer signed and convince both the bank and me that it would work financially, and if they could succeed in building out the renovation they proposed, they would be on their way to creating an increment of a lifetime income—an independent income in real estate.

How would they actually do the deal? Wellsley said they had talked to every bank in town, and not a single bank would touch it. The $800,000 foreclosure had made them all wary. They went back to Chapel Hill and had found a banker at First South who agreed to lend to them based on the "as will be" appraisal.

That was a new term to me. In the North, we called it the "as built" value. This meant that the bank would lend based on what the property would be worth once they were through the construction process and had it 100% rented. They had done a projection of construction costs and an income/expense statement based on their new rents, and the bank bought it. First South agreed to lend them $650,000 on the project. They said that First South typically lent on farmland in North Carolina and that they were the bank's first venture into diversifying its portfolio into real estate. Their banker had confided this as she issued their commitment letter on the loan.

The bank wanted to see 20% equity in the deal, or $130,000. Wellsley and Matt had told them about the $50,000 the owners had agreed to keep in second position. The bank agreed to apply that toward their equity requirement, but the bank still wanted to see that they had the balance in cash in the deal. They had their $5,000 cash, and what they needed from me, if I was willing, was a loan of $75,000 during the construction period. They would refinance the bank's loan after completion of the construction and rent up of the units and pay me back.

They had done their homework. They had researched the market from Virginia to South Carolina. They had looked at dozens of properties. They had applied the principles Frost and I taught them at the White Furniture Factory, and with input from us, they had developed financial tools and budgets for construction and operation of the project. They were young, smart, and energetic. I thought back to the early days of my career in real estate, and the financial support I had asked for and received from my father. Prior to his death, he had established a small trust for the benefit of the family. As the executor, I had the authority to lend them $75,000 from the family trust; together with their $5,000 and the second mortgage from the seller, that would give them the balance they needed. What better place to turn to for money than family, if it is available, and provided you have the discipline and character to pay it back. Lending them the money would get them started in their career. I was glad they had asked.

Wellsley and Matt finished the Courtyard renovation and rented it at $650 per unit as projected. After two and a half years of successful operation, they went back to the bank. With a new appraisal, the value shot up from $650,000 to $1.1 million based on the renovations and the increased rents they were receiving. They refinanced for $950,000, which was the final amount they had in the deal. They repaid the family trust and still had their $25,000-a-year cash flow from the property.

From their point of view, through their negotiations with the seller, with the bank, and with me, and with a lot of hard work on their part, they had been able to create an increment of a lifetime income with no cash of their own.

From my point of view, Wellsley and Matt were perfect examples of the Four D's. They had the Desire, the Drive, and the Discipline to lead to Delivery of an exceptional first project. In their late twenties, they were well on their way to creating an independent income in real estate.

CHAPTER 16

AN INDEPENDENT INCOME:
The Rewards of Personal Growth

---

*If, however, a man in a leading position applies the
limitations first to himself, demanding little from those
associated with him, and with modest means manages
to achieve something, good fortune is the result.*

Shortly after Wellsley and Matt had finished renovating
Courtyard Apartments, a local attorney called them. He had
observed their success with Courtyard, and he had a client
who wanted to sell them Moore Apartments, a similar project three blocks away. It was also very close to the center
of Burlington. The seller, the attorney said, was in his late
seventies. He had grown children, but they weren't interested in the project. It was thirty units, brick, with hardwood
floors, and rented mostly by unreliable tenants on month-to-
month leases. The seller's father had built it in the late 1920s,
and for nostalgic reasons, Wellsley told me, he wanted to see
the project put into the hands of people who would really
care for it, who would restore it to its original glory. He had
watched their renovation at Courtyard and had even come to
the opening-day party that, at my suggestion, Wellsley and
Matt held for the city in celebration of this first step. It was
a beginning step in the revitalization of downtown Burlington. The owner had observed them, and he wanted them to

have the property.

He was prepared to offer to sell them Moore Apartments for $385,000 for thirty units—an unbelievably low price at that time, given its location, but it had not been touched for sixty years. It was a wreck. One quarter of the job, Wellsley said, was just the cleanup factor. It was truly rundown, but again Wellsley and Matt were able to see through the filth, and the unreliable tenants, to the potential for the project.

How would they deal with the tenants in this project? At Courtyard, they had worked around many of the occupants, renovating the vacant units first, and eventually getting to the occupied units as the leases ran out. Here, she said, they decided that since there were no leases, and since every single unit was rented month to month, they would send a blanket letter giving the tenants thirty days to move.

Most of the tenants had moved out without any hassle. Wellsley and Matt ended up giving some leeway to a few people. One nice older couple had moved there when they were married forty years ago. Matt helped them move out. Nearby, he found a suitable one-story house for them, where they didn't have to climb three flights of stairs. He also gave them extra time to move. It had cost a bit more money, but Wellsley and Matt helped them.

Business is about more than just money. It is about service, caring, and human interaction. Wellsley and Matt were proving this for themselves.

By emptying the building of tenants rather than trying to work around them as apartments became vacant, the construction schedule would be a lot easier than Courtyard's. Having an empty building allowed them to replace the plumbing and the electrical system, redo the kitchens and bathrooms, reframe and install new sheet rock, sand and refinish the floors, and paint. They completed the apartments in sequence rather than jumping around thirty units, half of which might have been occupied.

By now, Matt was more experienced finding subcontractors and laborers; he was supervising a staff of fifteen to twenty workers at any one time. Wellsley and Matt's confidence had increased, due to their success with the first project, but it had not increased to the point of arrogance. They were still daunted by the prospects, that it was possible they could fail to complete the project before the bank's money ran out, or that they would be unable to rent the apartments once they were renovated. They had been successful renting Courtyard—to young professionals mostly—but they really had nothing more than their intuition to go on about the depth of the apartment market in Burlington. If they built it, would tenants come?

I asked how they had gone about financing Moore. Wellsley said the seller was friendly. He had liked them, but he was not willing to take back paper. He knew he was giving them a good deal selling it at $12,800 per unit, but he was not willing to hold a second mortgage. They had not owned Courtyard long enough at that time to refinance it and raise more cash, but the bank did allow them to use it as collateral security against Moore. The bank took a second mortgage on Courtyard. They agreed to lend them the money for the purchase and the renovations on Moore based again on the "as will be" value of the property and the added security of a second mortgage against their existing property.

Wellsley had done projections for the construction costs and figured out how much income and expenses they would have once the work was completed, and the property had rented. She said their favorite banker by then had moved from First South to Sun Trust. The banker liked them, and she trusted them. She sold the idea of Wellsley and Matt's new project to her credit committee. The bank agreed to lend them 100% of the deal—both the purchase price and renovation costs.

They thought they had it in the bag—until the bank put in a kicker. The bank wanted to see some money at risk. The bank wanted to see a total of $137,000 in Wellsley and Matt's account that would be drawn against for construction prior to the bank lending anything. So they had it, but they didn't have it. They had asked me, then, if I could help again. This time I agreed to personally lend them the $137,000 the bank was requiring. Once the project was complete, and the bank was satisfied, they would pay back my loan from the proceeds of the bank loan, which was already committed. It was a no-risk deal.

However, they ran into an unexpected opportunity as work began, and people came by to ask about the new apartments. They realized they had the potential of attracting a very strong, young professional tenant base into this, their second project.

As they talked to these potential tenants, they found that this clientele wanted washing machines and dryers in the apartments. Some of them had also suggested the idea of creating a pass-through from the kitchen into the dining room. Basically, the tenants wanted the units opened up a bit, and they wanted to be able to wash and dry their clothes without having to go to the local laundromat.

Given the level of clientele they were attracting to the building, Wellsley and Matt decided to upgrade the finishes on the kitchen cabinets and counters. They turned a spare closet into a laundry center. They reconfigured the units to make them larger by turning what was thirty small units into twenty-four more spacious units.

Their rental market loved it. They had the apartments rented before the work was completely done. People would sign leases to take effect upon completion of construction. But they were spending more than they had planned for and more than the bank had agreed to finance. They had a shortfall.

I agreed to keep my money in for a while. They talked to the bank. Their rent-roll numbers supported a slightly higher loan. Once they had finished the project and had it rented, they figured it would take a couple of more years before they would be able to refinance it for enough to repay their debt to me. They were in that process now. The bank had put in a prepayment penalty of 5% the first year, 3% the second year, and 1% the third year. This meant that if the loan were to be paid off in the first year, they would owe thousands of dollars in a penalty payment. Next January they would be able to refinance and pay me off and pay only the 1% prepayment penalty. In the meantime, both the bank and I were charging them interest only.

With the success of both Moore and Courtyard, Wellsley and Matt, still under thirty years old, had created a $50,000-a-year independent income for themselves. They had found an untapped market when they found Burlington.

They had been lucky, but they had created their own luck by their desire to expand into real estate, and by their drive and perseverance in looking for and finally finding two exceptionally risky, but exceptionally rewarding deals. Their second child was on the way.

At some level, it is the prospect of financial failure that forces each of us to focus all our energy on an activity. It is the prospect of having nothing to eat, no place to live, of having to move back in with our parents for survival, that moves us to take a job, to venture out into the work place, to somehow make it on our own. The rewards of personal growth, of earning our keep by service to others, giving others something they need, far outweigh the risks of doing nothing with our lives, of staying on the couch in front of the TV.

Whatever we do to propel ourselves into the workplace takes courage. At various times, some of us have more of it; some of us have less of it. But we choose a field; we take a job; and we are launched. Wellsley and Matt were succeeding at the most elemental level of real estate. On their own, they had found a project. They had figured out, with help from many people, and from the trial and error of offering on seven properties, how to negotiate the purchase and how to finance the deal. Using basic construction skills, Matt had figured out how to plan and run the renovation job. Together they had learned how to rent the apartments to tenants—basic friendliness and being willing to put yourself out there. It's not rocket science. You don't need an expensive education to do this. You simply need the desire. It begins with de-sire—perhaps a little bit of fear, as you follow the process, but without the desire, you never even begin. Desire leads almost automatically to Drive—you get to work! Discipline follows, for if you don't move methodically through the development process, you quickly realize you will never get to Delivery—the opening of your new project. The 4-Ds—Desire, Drive, Discipline—all lead to Delivery.

CHAPTER 17

WENDY AND LARRY'S SUCCESS:
No Cash, Just the Desire

Where such an example occurs,
it meets with emulation, so that whatever
is undertaken must succeed.

Wellsley's parents in Greensboro, North Carolina, had taken a different approach. Over the years, my brother-in-law Larry had developed a successful insurance brokerage. He and my sister Wendy had rented the ground floor of an attractive but run-down three-story building for his latest office relocation, directly across the street from the University of North Carolina at Greensboro. The upstairs was a rooming house for students. The downstairs was vacant and in need of a facelift. They cleaned, painted, did a few renovations, and turned the first floor into Larry's insurance office.

Wendy and Larry hadn't really considered buying real estate. They had watched me grow from a single-family property to hundreds of units. They owned a nice house in an upscale residential area of Greensboro, but the idea of owning and managing an income property hadn't crossed their minds. Their office was well located; they had done a nice job renovating it, but the entire building needed a facelift. Not only that, the roof had leaked repeatedly. After requesting numerous times that the landlord repair it, and after many failed attempts, both they and the landlord were disgusted with the situation.

Rather than repairing the roof properly, the landlord decided to list the building for sale. He asked a friend of his, a Realtor who worked primarily in Florida, to take the listing. The Realtor set the asking price at $250,000. The building sat. No one wanted it at that price. The Florida Realtor had brought his expertise from a different market and tried to apply it to Greensboro. He had created unrealistic expectations for the owner as to what his property was worth, and he had thereby alienated any potential buyer. The building continued to sit.

Undaunted, Larry worked out the income and expense numbers on the building. By checking around the neighborhood, he determined that the rents were at market for the condition of the building. If the building were renovated, he figured that the rents could be raised. Who paid the utilities? The owner. What would the building support after taxes, insurances, maintenance, and utilities? How much would they have to spend on a new roof and a facelift for the building? He and Wendy backed into the purchase price. They prepared a written offer for $95,000. That was their estimate of the value of the building. Given the work that had to be done to bring the building up to their standards—that was what the rents from the upper floors, plus the rent from their office, would support. By then, the owner was totally discouraged at the lack of interest in his $250,000 building, and he accepted their offer of $95,000. Larry let the seller negotiate the price up to $97,500, more as a face-saving, feel-good issue for the seller than a reflection of the value. As soon as the offer was signed and they had put down a deposit, Larry found that "everybody in town wanted to buy this building." He felt he had gotten a good deal.

Unbeknownst to Larry and my sister when they purchased it, the building turned out to be in a HUD target area for redevelopment. The Department of Housing and Urban Development would make a secondary loan for improvements to the property. The HUD administrator visited the property and told them they needed to move in a hurry, for if the money was not spent in that calendar year, it would go back to the government. Wendy and Larry got to work immediately, putting their package together—getting estimates on the roof replacement, the plumbing, wiring, and basic remodeling they planned to do on the interior. They turned in their completed application to HUD, and within a few weeks, HUD agreed to give them a second mortgage on the property to cover the cost of their repairs and upgrades. A local bank lent them the money for the purchase. With an additional small bridge loan from Wendy's and my father, they were able to buy the building and renovate it with no money of their own in the deal. They spent $75,000 on renovations, plus $97,500 for the purchase, so they ended up with a total of $172,500 in the property.

Once it was completed with new aluminum siding, a new roof, and the interior renovations, and once it was rented at the increased rents for the new eight-bedroom student apartment they had created on the upper floors, the bank refinanced the building. Wendy and Larry paid off the bridge loan to our father with money left from the bank and HUD financing. They now owned their office and several income-producing apartments on the upper two floors. They found that the monthly cost was no more than the cost of the utilities for the building. They now owned their office, essentially rent-free.

Not only was their office rent-free, but they found they had enjoyed the process. They had enjoyed figuring out the value of the project and negotiating the deal with the seller. They had enjoyed designing and planning the renovations, and Larry had particularly enjoyed supervising the workers and subcontractors that had done the work on the building.

Wendy was an artist in Greensboro and had painted many murals for local banks, as well as a mural half a city block long on the exterior of an important building downtown, all part of a downtown revitalization plan. She also painted portraits on a regular basis. Larry had envied her creative outlet, and he had now found an outlet for his own creativity in the purchase and renovation of a building—a nice addition to running his insurance business.

Larry took the lead and began looking around the area for their second property. Two elderly sisters owned a building next door to the office. They had lived there for more than forty years, and Wendy and Larry had become friends with them. One morning, Larry read in the paper that one of the sisters had died. He went to calling hours, and after a few weeks, during which time he and Wendy did a lot of market research in the area—simply knocking on doors that had for-rent signs and asking what people paid for rents, he approached the surviving sister about the possibility of purchasing her house. It was an elegant house. She had lived there most of her adult life. It turned out that with the death of her sister, she was ready to move on. She told Larry she had a nephew who had expressed interest in the property, but she didn't think he was in a position to purchase it.

Larry made an offer in which she would hold a second mortgage. Not only would she get cash from the first mortgage which Larry and Wendy would obtain from the bank, but she would also have an income for the next twenty-five or thirty years, probably for as long as she lived, from the balance of the purchase price, which she agreed to hold in a second mortgage. Larry had analyzed the layout of the house and figured out they could turn it into three large apartments. Running the numbers on the property with the rent from the apartments, they knew they could pay all expenses and have money left over.

The bank bought their concept and lent based on the "as will be" value of the property, which was enough to cover the purchase price and the renovation costs. The bank did require a 20% down payment on the deal, but the second mortgage that the surviving sister agreed to hold provided that.

I asked Larry if the bank knew about the second mortgage, and he told me they never asked. His attorney had prepared the offer in two pages. The first offer was for $85,000 for the building. This they gave to the bank. The second page was the arrangement with the seller to hold the second mortgage. At the closing, they had closed the bank loan, and after the bank representative left their attorney's office, they closed the second mortgage with the seller. The bank was in first position. They were secure. Nothing in their loan documents prohibited secondary financing against the building. The cash flow was enough to cover both mortgages and give them a positive income—besides, the bank had never asked about a second mortgage, and Larry had never brought it up.

Larry said that if they had asked, he would of course have told them about it. That might have meant bank refusal to lend on the property, but as often as not, banks at that time were not concerned about secondary financing so long as their mortgage was no more than 75%-80% of the purchase price, or the appraised value of the improved property.

Wendy and Larry invited the surviving sister to the property, once during the renovation process and again at the end of the job, when the building had been converted into three apartments. She toured the building and complimented them on the job they had done. "You did honor to the property," she told them. Her elegant home had been turned into a three-bedroom apartment with a bathroom for each bedroom, a four-bedroom apartment with a bathroom for each bedroom, and a studio or efficiency apartment. The bedrooms were huge. Larry had furnished it with attractive but used furniture he picked up from various auctions held around town. Wendy and Larry now owned their second income property, and they had done it again with no cash of their own.

The surviving sister's nephew came up to them afterwards. "I figured out what you did," he complained to Larry. "You bought my aunt's house with no money of your own. You've got nothing in it, and now you own it!"

Larry smiled and said, "That's right, but we did the work."

"I could have done that, if I'd had the guts," said the nephew, and he turned and walked away.

Another neighbor in the area called Larry. He had

noticed the job they had done renovating their office building. He was ready to leave town and move to California. Would they like to buy his four-unit property? Larry analyzed the deal. By now, he knew the market in the area. If the building were improved, there was room to raise the rents. It needed painting and new furniture. Larry offered the neighbor $142,000 and presented the bank with the revised income and expense statement he felt confident he could achieve. The neighbor accepted the offer. Again, the bank agreed to lend a first mortgage based on the value of the improved property, which would be $161,000. They agreed to lend 80%, or $128,800. The seller agreed to hold a second mortgage of $20,000. Larry spent $6,000 on a paint job and new furniture from the auctions. He and Wendy had walked away from that deal with $7,000 in their pocket and had a building that would produce a few hundred dollars a month extra cash flow.

Wendy and Larry repeated this process seventeen times. Larry kept selling insurance, Wendy kept up with her artwork, and year after year, they kept improving their income by purchasing houses close to the university, houses they would buy typically with a combination of bank and owner financing, and houses that would provide, once each one was cleaned up, painted, and possibly reconfigured, an increment of a lifetime income.

Wendy and Larry had been very successful, and in the process, they developed their own set of guidelines for buying real estate:

1. Do your own hands-on personal market research in your area. Be realistic about the rents you can charge.

2. Don't like the property; like the numbers.
3. Be willing to turn any offer loose if the numbers don't work.
4. Don't believe real estate people who tell you that you have to lose money on properties in the beginning. Negotiate deals that generate cash flow from the outset. It is possible to do.
5. In buying older buildings, there are always hidden costs. Get experienced contractors to quote the cost of renovations so that you are presenting numbers to the bank that you can live with. You may or may not choose to use the contractor for the renovation, but if you are working with numbers from a contractor, you will probably be safe.
6. Negotiate to end up with cash up front through a combination of bank and seller financing. It will make a nice cushion, so long as the rent amounts will support the debt load.
7. Don't kid yourself about the numbers.
8. One of the most satisfying parts of owning real estate is not giving the government such a large percentage of your income in taxes.
9. Never calculate depreciation into your calculation of cash flow. Let the savings in taxes be an additional bonus.
10. Out of the seventeen houses they bought, only two have been purchased through Realtors. Keep your eyes open. Read the classifieds. Look for "For Sale by Owner" signs posted in the yards.
11. Allow sixty to seventy days from acceptance of the

offer to closing. Get permission to enter the house during that time and use that free period to rent the property on a "picture and a promise" of what it will look like once renovated.

12. Always make your purchase offer contingent upon "financing satisfactory to the buyer," and make it with a heavy second mortgage from the seller. If the property doesn't rent in the time between acceptance and closing, simply walk away.

CHAPTER 18

AN OBSESSION:
Getting the Picture, Making It Happen

If one is too severe in setting up restrictions,
people will not endure them. The more consistent such severity,
the worse it is, for in the long run a reaction is unavoidable.

It was the summer of 2010. At 12,000 feet, the rarified air of the High Sierras in central California leaves you gulping for oxygen as your body adjusts to the altitude. It took me a couple of days in the mountain peaks to return to breathing normally. Chuck (forty-nine), Locke (seventy-eight), and I (having just turned sixty-five) had packed in on mules—something Locke had done for the past twenty years—Ida, Sadie, and Evan. Mules are the most stubborn yet steady creatures known to man. Having ridden both, I'd rather ride a mule than a horse any day on the mountain trails. Our packer, Jim, rode the lead mule and led three pack animals, loaded side to side with all our gear. Locke followed Jim, and Chuck and I followed Locke, peering over each precipice with feigned unconcern as we rounded the hairpin turns on the slow climb into the granite peaks.

It took eight hours, but we finally arrived at Locke's campsite. The packer left us, and we spent ten days camping by a stream above the timberline in a wide, grassy basin, surrounded ten miles around, by sheer cliffs of granite.

We pitched our tents a hundred yards apart and had lots of alone time. We took day hikes into the peaks. We exhausted ourselves and grew stronger with the challenge. Locke had packed into this secret campsite for twenty years, and he swore the packers never brought anyone else here. Jim, the packer, had confirmed Locke's claim.

Chuck and Locke raced motorcycles. Even at seventy-eight years old, Locke was spry and strong. Together they owned a racing company that Chuck managed. Arc-Light Racing, Chuck told me, was sponsored by Suzuki. For sixteen years, he had managed his riders, tuned their engines to the max, and raced successfully. Arc-Light Racing was one of the few profitable racing firms in the country. Chuck had raced for sixteen years, and he and his stable of riders had brought home sixteen national championships.

On the twelfth and final turn at the Atlanta speedway last year, Chuck was following a thirty-year-old whirlwind racer, brushing up on his technique, and as he came down the straight at 170 mph, he slowed for the turn as he knew to do—leaned the bike onto his kneepad against the pavement, held the throttle steady, and watched as his lead bike gunned out of the turn a split second before he could. Chuck said he knew what he should do to maximize his speed coming out of the turn, but he just couldn't bring himself to hit the throttle full-bore in time. He lost a full second by his hesitation. It was then he knew, he said, that his racing days were over. Locke enjoyed just plugging around the track at 120 miles an hour for fun now, but Chuck, when he couldn't match the speed and performance of the thirty-year-old racer leading him through the track, knew it was time to close down Arc-Light and move on. Suzuki had cut back on their sponsorship budget this year, and it was just time.

Locke stayed in camp most days, while Chuck and I hiked on the peaks—sometimes together, sometimes alone. Chuck brought the same discipline to hiking that he had brought to racing. He was in top condition and could climb for hours at a time without taking a break. I moved more slowly, resting often and still adjusting to the puny oxygen levels at our altitude. We caught up together now and then and began talking; Chuck talked about racing; I talked about real estate. We returned to camp and continued talking. We talked continually for days.

Chuck, an engineer, was not one to do something without planning and thinking it through thoroughly. He told me he had considered his next move might be starting a series of Jiffy Lube franchises. He had a friend who had done it. He felt he could be successful at it. He had $100,000 saved from his racing. It was an impressive amount. When he heard that I owned income property, he wanted to hear everything about it. How does one get started? How does one find the properties? Did they make money right away? How much cash did it take to get in? How much time does it take to manage them?

Getting started is not difficult, I told Chuck. The California market was a stranger to me, but there is always something for sale. People's circumstances change; they grow older and want to sell their property. They take a job somewhere else. They die. There is always property available. I gave him the get-in-the-car speech. Drive around. Find out where you might want to buy.

Chuck lived in Lafayette, California, slightly rural compared to the coastal cities. He thought that might be a better place than San Francisco or Palo Alto to start, although he also knew those markets. Drive around Lafayette, I suggested. Look at the for-sale signs. Call Realtors. Look through the classifieds in your local paper. Talk to friends. Begin networking. Let people know you are interested in buying income property. It won't take long, before you will have identified one or more properties that might be suitable.

He listened to my New York City story of net-leasing a vacant brownstone and turning it into apartments. He heard about my first purchase; a buddy who let me simply take over his payments so he could leave town. He heard about borrowing against one property to purchase another. For me, somehow each property had just come along. The process had moved forward step by step. It was not difficult. It just took having the initial desire and figuring out the financing, and if he had that much money saved, it shouldn't be difficult to get started. I assured Chuck that once you have the desire and the direction, things just open up. Look at the way his motorcycle company had prospered.

Chuck was not shy. In no uncertain terms, he told me he figured his motorcycle company had prospered from his own hard work and planning. He had known what he wanted. He had wanted to make money racing. He knew how to tune engines. He knew how to hire and keep the best racers. He said he had learned as he went along, but it hadn't just happened. He had made it happen.

It was no different with real estate, I assured him. He didn't know the field yet, but he was asking the right questions and

206

starting to learn about it. He was thinking about it and beginning to envision how it could create an independent income for himself. The next step, when he got back home, would be to find his first property. It takes time. It takes focus and work, just like his motorcycle business, but it is not difficult, and it will likely become an obsession of sorts.

After you buy your first property, you realize you can do this. You learn how to find the properties through friends, Realtors, the classifieds. You learn how to "tune them up" to make the most money. Eventually, you learn how to hire staff and manage them, much as you did your racers. It doesn't "just happen." You make it happen. But it is not some esoteric endeavor. It is easy to learn, and with each property you buy, you are creating an increment of a lifetime income. Chuck only needed to apply the same brains, drive, and stamina toward real estate as he had to his motorcycle racing, and he would quickly see the results as he created an independent income in real estate. It works. He would see.

Chuck had listened. He began to see that this was indeed something at which he could be successful. We talked about how to price the rents—that he should make calls and look at other apartments in the area. Pretend he is a renter and go see what types of apartments landlords were offering and at what price. After three or four visits, he would have a pretty good idea of what was available in his area. He should find his first building. Add up the rents it will bring in. Subtract out the expenses for taxes, insurance, management, and maintenance. What's left will cover debt service to the bank and a return to him. He should buy an amortization book or find an amortization table on the internet or in Excel.

It will calculate the payment for a mortgage of any amount and at any interest rate and term. The local taxes he could find at the assessor's office or online; for insurance, he could call his broker. Management—he could rent the apartments himself; he could take care of any problems tenants have and pay the bills, just like he did with his personal budget and residence. It would not be difficult. It might take many false starts, many offers, but eventually he would find a property. He hadn't won every race he had ever entered either. He acknowledged that.

He should try to find a building with a problem, and I laid out Wellsley and Matt's story—buying a vacant rundown property for a fraction of the cost of a new property, fixing it up, and now living on the results of their work, ready to continue expanding. Chuck said he was sure prices in North Carolina didn't begin to compare with prices in California. "Prices in California must be absurdly high compared to North Carolina," he said.

They probably were, but he should keep looking. Prices are a function of income. A property can't be worth more than it can support. A seller may be asking for the moon but show him the numbers and negotiate it down to a realistic price, otherwise move on and find another. Eventually you will find a property. You don't buy an income property for pride, as you might your own personal residence. You buy it to make money, and I told him of Larry's office building, of a Florida Realtor trying to apply Florida pricing to Greensboro, North Carolina. Eventually, through Larry's negotiation and refusal to accept an absurdly high asking price, a $250,000 asking price became a $97,500 purchase price. Prices in Lafayette were probably lower than San Francisco, since it was forty miles outside the city.

I promised to send him purchase offers, budgets, and leases that I had developed (see Appendices) and offered to talk him through his first property once he got back home. As he saw the potential for creating an independent income in real estate, the Jiffy Lube franchise had faded into the background. One of the nicest things about income property—the property is sitting there making money for you, while you are on a trip like this in the High Sierras.

Ten days after we had arrived, our packer, Jim, showed up at the campsite with Ida, Sadie, Evan, and the other pack mules. We loaded our gear, mounted up, and descended the winding trail back to the pack station at a more breathable altitude. I had learned a passel about motorcycle racing; Chuck had learned a passel about real estate and was inspired to venture into creating his own independent income.

Weeks later, after I had returned to Ithaca, Chuck called me. He had found a twenty-unit apartment complex in the Lafayette area. His brother, a dentist, had agreed to put up $300,000. Together they had $400,000 to invest. Prices were high, but he thought they could do it. Family, friends, partners, whatever it takes to put the deal together; Chuck was getting the picture.

CHAPTER 19

DAVE'S SUCCESS:
From Laid-Off to Riches

In the same way,
the tormented body will rebel
against excessive asceticism.

On Thanksgiving Day, my brother-in-law Dave and his family drove down from Rochester to visit us at our home on Cayuga Lake. Dave had worked for twenty-six years as an engineer at Eastman Kodak. In the last ten years, Kodak had laid off over 30,000 employees from their work force. In this digital age, the demand for film had dwindled from a steady stream to a trickle. Early that September it was Dave's turn. He was cut from his division. He was the least senior of a dozen guys, many of whom had been working there for over thirty years, and as the least senior worker of the group, he was the first to be let go.

Dave was looking lean and gaunt. Every word from his mouth was negative. "I'm fifty-two—no one hires you at fifty-two. They see only ten or fifteen years left in you. You're not worth training." He was down and out. His wife, Cheryl, worked in the library at the local community college. His son had a job at the *Democrat and Chronicle*, Rochester's newspaper. Dave was unemployed for the first time in twenty-six years.

Over dinner, Carol suggested perhaps he should think

about real estate as a way to make money. He and Cheryl had run a large apartment complex when they were students at Syracuse University. Dave heard the suggestion but just shook his head. After dinner as we stood in the entryway saying our good-byes, I followed up on this idea with Dave and suggested he might think about finding an old house or some income property and fixing it up. He was a hard worker. He had the basic skills. He had done a remodeling job on his own house. He was intelligent and handy, and he did have the experience from his college days.

I offered to help him look for something. He should just let me know if this was an idea that might interest him. He shook my hand, and as he left, I saw the first glimmer of hope I had seen in his eyes that day.

The next day, Dave e-mailed me, thanking me for my offer of help and telling me that he had been thinking about what he needed to do, now that he was among the ranks of the unemployed. He thought he could survive for about two years on what he had saved in his IRA without working full time, but he was concerned. It would not be easy, and he would like to take me up on my offer. In fact, he was ready to go as soon as possible. Dave had taken the bait. He had begun to see a way out. It sounded like he had the Desire.

He continued sending emails with plenty of questions. He wanted to make the best use of my time. He wanted to know some examples of what to look for and where to look. He wanted to know what steps he needed to take if he did find a property. Was there anything he could do in advance that would allow him to move quicker, if a property did come along?

He said that Cheryl had always been skeptical about venturing out on their own, but with my offer of help, she seemed agreeable.

He wanted also to include their son, who at twenty-three was struggling to find his way in the world. Dave said his son was young, strong, and capable. He just needed experience working with tools and gaining more confidence in what he could do. He said his son had good insights about the market in various areas of the city, and he had a flair for design. They got along well, and Dave felt they would make a good team. Before being laid off, Dave said he had been urging his son to buy a multifamily home—a "rat" that needed fixing up.

Reading his e-mail, my mind began summarizing what I had been recommending to people for years: what to look for, what steps to take if you find a property, what to do in advance to allow you to move more quickly if a property comes along.

I emailed back to Dave that he should get in his car, drive around the area, and look for a property that seems interesting. Call the Realtor or look up the owner at the courthouse. Just get inside the house somehow. Get a tour, ask for the numbers—rents, expenses. Go to his local bank. Find out what the terms are for commercial mortgages, because an income property is considered commercial, not residential and the interest rate will likely be higher.

The next day, Dave wrote back—he had found a single-family house in the outskirts of Rochester. He had toured through it. It was indeed run-down, but he felt he could do all the work needed to bring it back to rentable condition. He was excited. He could pick it up for under

$80,000. The owner said he might finance enough for the down payment—even up to $20,000 of the purchase price. Would I come up and look at with him?

Responding, I asked Dave how much it would cost to renovate the house. It was a three-bedroom, and he thought he could paint it and fix it up for perhaps another $10,000. He would have $90,000 invested, if he used the owner's offer of $20,000 as the down payment. Pulling out my calculator—$90,000 at 6.5% interest over a 25-year period would cost him $580.64/month or $6,967.69 annually; taxes probably $3,600 per year—or $300/month; insurance $600—or $50 per month. Maintenance, Dave would do himself, but he would need to buy supplies, probably another $600 annually—$50/month. Utilities would probably be paid by the tenant. Dave's monthly expenses on the single-family three-bedroom house would run about $400 per month plus debt service of $580—$980 per month overall cost. Dave thought the house would rent for $1,200 to $1,300 per month. Using my estimates for expenses, if the house were 100% financed, we calculated he would make between $200 and $300 per month, and that was setting nothing aside for major improvements or vacancies.

We talked it over on the phone. If he withdrew $20,000 from his IRA for the down payment, he would eliminate $108 per month from his debt service, and he might make $300 to $400 per month total. How long would it take him to renovate the house and put it into rentable condition? He thought he could do it over two to three months, although he would have to wait for warmer weather to paint the exterior. He said he realized he would have to cover the debt service, taxes, insurance, and winter heat while he worked on it.

Dave was excited about the prospect of starting to work right away. He was beginning to exhibit the Drive that he would need to do a deal. I didn't want to discourage him, but tried to put this in perspective for him, suggesting that if he renovated the house and were able to rent it within three months, it would likely make him a little money. If he had a bad tenant, someone who was unable to pay the rent, he would be stuck. Would $300 a month be worth the risk and the effort? It was a start, he thought. He could handle it—the single-family house.

I was willing to come up and look at it with him, but perhaps he should consider the following: With a single-family house, he would have one roof, one boiler, one yard to keep up, one set of books to keep, and he would have one tenant to pay for it all. If that tenant lost his job, or walked away from his lease, Dave would lose 100% of his income and still have all the expenses for taxes, insurance, utilities, and debt service he would have to pay, and he would have no other income to cover these costs.

However, with a multifamily house, say six to ten units or more, typically he would still have one roof, one boiler, one yard to keep up, one set of books to keep, and he would have six to ten tenants to pay for it all. If one tenant failed, he would still have five to nine tenants continuing to pay the rent.

In addition, it would take him approximately the same amount of time to find, close on, and assimilate a ten-unit apartment building into his portfolio as it would a single-family house. A ten-unit property would surely cost more, but it would require the same negotiation with the owner, the same negotiation with the bank, the same book-keeping system, and basically the same time commitment to manage and rent as would a single-family house. But it could also produce a net income to Dave ten times that of a single-family house. Would his time be better spent on the smaller project or in finding a larger one? He saw my point. He could handle the purchase and the work on a single-family house, but he would look further and call me once he found something larger to show me.

A week later, Dave called. He had found a fifty-one-unit building near where he used to work. He had talked with a neighbor who used to manage the property, who said it used to be for sale for $1.4 million. The owner was out of town. It was a lot of money, but Dave thought that if the owner was willing to negotiate on the price, and if he would hold a second mortgage, perhaps he could make it work. It was a big step for him, but it sounded reasonable, and I agreed to come up and look at the property. In the meantime, he should talk to the owner, get the rents, and see it for himself.

I was impressed. Dave was no longer thinking small. He had quickly shifted gears. He had left behind his infatuation with the single-family home. Fifty-one units, if bought right and fixed up, he figured, could support a family. How would he raise the money? We hadn't gotten that far yet. If the owner was willing to finance it, that was a start. He'd need some cash. He and Cheryl had lived frugally during his twenty-six years at Kodak. They had money saved, and they owned their house outright. Would they be willing to use their savings, or would they be willing to refinance their house and raise a couple of hundred thousand dollars for a down payment? That was a huge step. Giving up the security of money in the bank and a house paid off was a lot to ask of oneself and one's family. On the other hand, having no job, no income, was a terrible thing to face.

Dave had to weigh the risks. How could he find other sources of cash? His father and mother were not well off. They had raised seven kids on the salary of an IBM tool-and-die maker and a substitute teacher. All their kids were grown and married. They were comfortable now, but Dave probably could not go to them for a down payment. What about other friends or siblings? Would the property support 100% financing? In other words, if the owner or a bank would lend him, say 80% of $1.4 million, Dave would have to come up with $280,000 cash to do the deal. Not only would he have to pay debt service on the remaining $1,120,000, but also on the $280,000. The only way he would know would be to analyze the rents, look at the leases, and see if they were for real, see how many people were paying and what was the actual rent roll, not just the one on paper. If the property was as run-down as he indicated, it probably did not have the highest quality tenants; many of them probably didn't pay. It would only be by running the "real numbers" that Dave would be able to determine whether the property was worth $1.4 million.

We discussed all this over the phone and made arrangements to meet in Rochester. By the time I got there the following week, Dave had already made friends with the property manager, who had an office on the first floor. The property manager had told him the property had been listed for sale for over a year, but she wasn't sure whether the owner still wanted to sell or not. She had taken Dave through some typical units, including the garage and basement.

Dave was excited. He had figured out the numbers on a first pass, based on what the property manager told him were typical rents—a one-bedroom rented for $400 and a two for $500. There was an equal number of ones and twos. Fifty units (at least one will usually be vacant) at $450 per month average = $22,500 per month gross rent, or $270,000 per year. From the amortization book he had bought, Dave figured that in order to cover $1.4 million of debt service, at 6% interest, over twenty-five years, the cost would be $8,991 per month, or $107,892 annually. Based on the rule of thumb I gave him, he figured expenses would run about 40% of gross income or $108,000 annually. He had set a target for himself of making around $3,000 per month from the property. He wanted to earn no less than $36,000 per year. It wasn't as much as he made at Kodak, but it was a start.

Adding debt service of $107,892, expenses of $108,000, and the $36,000 he wanted to make, the total was $251,892. He could make his $36,000 a year and still have a cushion of $18,108 for vacancy and major repairs. This property seemed worthwhile! In addition, now to Desire and Drive, Dave was showing he had the Discipline to create a financial structure.

This was all a preliminary first pass. It assumed no equity in the deal—only borrowed money. It assumed paying full asking price. And it assumed expenses running about 40%. Dave would still have to do his "due diligence" on the property and get the exact rents and the exact expenses, but at this point, he had a pretty good idea of what the property might be worth to him. I returned home, satisfied that Dave had found a possible first deal, providing it was actually for sale.

He got the address of the owners from the property manager. They lived in New Jersey. He had a friend who was an attorney, and he met with him and asked him to draw up a purchase offer. Human nature being what it is, Dave had him write up the purchase offer for a $1.1 million sale price. He figured the owner would probably want to negotiate, so he left room to add to the purchase price. It turned out Dave was ahead of himself. He had the offer drawn up and then called the owner in New Jersey to tell him he had toured the property and had a purchase offer prepared. The owner thanked him but informed him that he and his partners had decided to take their property off the market.

Dave called me. He was disappointed but not discouraged. He was beginning to learn the lesson of non-attachment to outcomes in this business of real estate. You find a property. You analyze it. You put your best foot forward. But you don't let yourself be devastated if a deal doesn't work out. I encouraged Dave to keep looking. There are millions of deals out there, and I assured him one of them was meant for him.

He bounced back. We arranged a meeting with a broker friend of mine at NorthMarq Capital. I had done a number of deals through them. My broker friend knew a contractor who had forty townhouses for sale. Dave got printouts of the offering and looked at the numbers. They were expensive! They were just built, were fully rented, and could be bought for $150,000 each. The problem was there was no problem. Even if Dave could figure out the financing of a $6 million project for his first one, not only would it take over $1.2 million in cash to buy them, but there would be no immediate upside. They were perfect. They were brand new. They were fully leased, and of course the owner wanted top dollar.

This was a project for a wealthy individual who had money to park in a real estate investment and was looking a return better than what he could get in a tax-exempt bond or even in the stock market. For someone looking to create value immediately, there was no upside to be realized from solving a problem. Not only was this project too big for Dave to get his arms around, it was simply not the right project for creating immediate upside through renovation and the solving of a problem, and that was what he needed.

Dave kept looking. He found a Realtor that he liked, and the Realtor began sending him sales sheets on income properties he had listed. Dave called me to tell me that through his Realtor friend, he had found forty-four units in two locations that could be purchased as a package. They were older buildings built in the 1930s, and they could be picked up for around $30,000 per unit. Dave had been through them, and if the city would allow it, there was a basement with windows only half below grade that could be converted into two apartments. He could do the conversion and raise the value immediately.

I drove to Rochester for a meeting. We met on the front stoop of a classic two-story brick building with limestone decorative elements over the entrance. Dave's Realtor and the Realtor for the seller were with him. The owners, we were told, were two young guys who had made a fortune buying and selling local real estate. They were moving on to larger projects, and they wanted to sell the forty-four units to raise additional cash for them to move forward. Again, Dave was excited. The property was old, but it was sound. It had hardwood floors, which were level. The superintendent had a small unit and took care of the property. We went into a couple of vacant units. Dave would be able to paint, upgrade the appliances and some of the bathroom and kitchen fixtures, and create more desirable units for a slightly higher-class clientele, who would likely pay a higher rent. The basement did indeed present a great opportunity for adding two units of income to his rent roll. Dave said that the other building was similar, and even though it was halfway across town, he would be able to care for them both without a problem.

Dave ran through his due diligence over the next two weeks. Finally, with the help of his attorney friend, he was ready to submit a purchase offer. He offered $1.2 million with $100,000 down (from his IRA). He would assume the owners' first mortgage for $800,000, and the owners would hold the balance of $300,000 in a second mortgage.

His Realtor spoke to the seller's Realtor and said that Dave should submit the offer. Dave had calculated he could make $50,000 a year on the deal.

Unfortunately, the sellers had anticipated being able to have a buyer assume their first mortgage. The bank would have none of it. Dave would have to find his own financing, and the seller's mortgage would have to be paid off. However, the sellers would incur a significant prepayment penalty to pay off their mortgage. They had borrowed against these properties when rates were 8%. If the bank had to place that money at the current going rate of 6%, it would cost them a considerable amount. The way their mortgage was written, the mortgagor would have to cover the difference, and it amounted to several hundred thousand dollars. The sellers had not realized their problem when they listed their property. Now that they did, they took it off the market. Dave had wasted months on this one, but that was the way it was. Dave had the Desire, the Drive, and the Discipline, but he was beginning to wonder if he would ever own a piece of real estate.

Buy a problem. That had been my approach to purchasing real estate. Dave finally found a problem of his own. When he told me about it and asked me to come up and see it, I was skeptical. It was a twenty-unit property, located in a questionable but possibly up-and-coming part of town. It was mostly filled with social-service tenants, renting month to month, which in my experience was not a good indication of stability. Dave might have some problem collecting rents on a regular basis, which of course would negatively affect his cash flow.

The property was run-down, but Dave felt certain he could paint and repair each unit as it became vacant. I looked at it, and remembered some of the burned-out, run-down properties I had started with. He had definitely found a problem. But it was one he could buy with his own resources and he would find his own way through it. Dave did buy it.

His attorney worked out an arrangement whereby he could utilize the assets in his Kodak IRA account. If he were to withdraw them outright, he would be taxed at over 15%. He could, however, lend them to someone else as an investment without being taxed. Dave worked out a loan to his sister. She re-lent the funds back to Dave. She paid the loan to his IRA every month and Dave paid back the loan to her from the proceeds of the property. It worked. It turned out his mom did have funds, but rather than investing them and becoming an owner, she lent them to him, and he paid her a monthly interest payment. This fit her plans nicely, as it gave her some additional income each month. With a 20% down payment in place, he had no problem securing bank financing on a first mortgage.

The first month, Dave found he had to replace the boiler. He had been going to HVAC School at the community college, paid for by his job relocation plan with Kodak, so he was able to do the work himself. He painted. He refinished floors. He learned how to evict deadbeat tenants. He found out that the previous manager had been pocketing much of the rent and simply telling the owner that people hadn't paid. Within a year, Dave had the building cleaned up, had gotten rid of most of his problem tenants, had made friends with the building inspector, had won the respect of his banker—he was truly launched on his real estate career.

He met and made friends with Harry, his aging neighbor who owned twenty-seven units across the street from Dave's property. Harry was ninety years old and due for a hip replacement. Dave first offered to buy his property, but Harry did not want to sell. This place was his life. So then Dave offered to manage it for him for a fee of 5% of the rents. He also did the maintenance and got paid for that. Harry had his hips replaced and relied more than ever on Dave. Harry's son would inherit the property and he assured Dave that he would allow him to buy it once Harry was gone.

In the meantime, Dave responded to an ad for a property up the street—"For Sale by Owner." Eight units in a bright purple house were for sale. He went through it and found it to be in perfect order. No problem here; however, the owner was willing to finance it himself, with only a 10% down payment. This would give the owner a monthly income and make it easier for someone like Dave to buy it without having to go to the bank. Dave ran the numbers. They worked. And he then did the same deal with his IRA—his sister borrowed from the IRA and re-lent it to Dave, who paid her back monthly, and he bought the eight units.

At this point, Dave's real estate career spanned two years from when he had been let go from Kodak. His attitude had totally reversed from that Thanksgiving Day at our house two years ago. He was enthusiastic. He enjoyed being his own boss. He felt successful and independent. Dave sent me an email one day, thanking me for my assistance and telling me that with his new acquisition of eight units, his original property of twenty units, and managing Harry's twenty-seven units across the street, he now had enough money to live on. He was continuing to look for new real estate opportunities. Dave was indeed launched.

CHAPTER 20

THE FOUR Ds:
Desire, Drive, Discipline & Delivery

On the other hand, although ruthless severity is not to be applied persistently and systematically, there may be times when it is the only means of safeguarding against guilt and remorse...

Ithaca is a small town of 30,000. Though small, it maintains an open window to the world through Cornell University. Students come here from all fifty states and over a hundred countries. The Statler Hotel School, the Johnson Business School, and the more recent Cornell Baker Program in Real Estate are among the university schools that attract this international group of students. All three schools maintain an exceptional faculty and attract a stable of world-class lecturers. Students will leave Cornell to run some of the major corporations and businesses of the world. Not everyone, however, will be a world leader. There is still room for the student who will return to small-town Iowa to run the family business, or start their own business from the bottom, and work their way up to a fortune and success. It is probably for these students that I am occasionally invited to lecture—as the local small-town real estate developer.

The principles of creating income in real estate are similar, however, whether you are developing hundreds of acres of a new subdivision in California, building a new hotel in

Singapore, renovating an office building in Manhattan, or buying your first income property in Schenectady. They all require the four Ds: Desire, Drive, Discipline, and Delivery. Why are you getting involved in real estate in the first place? Each one of us has a Desire for more—more and more. Real estate income property can fulfill that Desire for more money, more accomplishment, and more success. We begin the subdivision, the hotel, the office building, or simply the purchase of our first small property with the Desire for more financial success.

Very seldom do things work out exactly as we anticipate. There are twists and turns along the way. But we keep moving along the path. We just take it as it comes. The seller of the land or building wants too much money. The banks won't lend all the money we need. We must find more equity for a down payment. The land turns out to be a "brown-field" (toxic waste clean-up required) and will require remediation. The market is questionable. We're not sure we will be able to rent it or sell it once it is built. There are a thousand roadblocks to developing a new project or purchasing an existing property. You have the Desire for more, but without the Drive to make a project happen, you will collapse by the roadside in disappointment at every obstacle. We look around, and we think, "Building a building must be easy. There are so many houses and buildings that have been built. Who can do it? Who has all the money to make a project happen? Not you. Not me ..."

The ones who can do it, the ones who can succeed in buying a building, or building a building, are the ones who have the Desire and the Drive to make it happen. They commit to a project, and they work through every obstacle to purchase, every obstacle to the renovation or construction of a building, until it is completed, until it is as perfect as they can make it given the restrictions of time and resources. They find the money. They clean up the site. They design a project that will fit the market, and they find a bank that will cooperate within the parameters of the project. The ones who build, renovate, and own buildings are the ones with the Desire and the Drive to make it happen.

Discipline is the personal strength to hold your tongue as your rage boils away inside when the banker changes the loan terms at the last minute, or the seller raises his price for the third time even though you thought you had an agreement; it's important to have the Discipline not to burn bridges. You need the Discipline to budget for construction and stick to it—to receive that first draw from the bank and apply it to the project, not to the vacation to the Bahamas, or the new boat you've been dreaming about, which can be very tempting. You need the Discipline to stay with the project and visit your crews who are working overtime until 2:00 a.m. or all-day Sunday to meet your deadline. You need Discipline to advertise, market, and lease or sell your soon-completed product so that it will be filled within days or weeks of opening. You will quickly realize the Discipline it takes to properly manage and care for your property and tenants, whether it is you alone, or your hired staff who do the work. And if you don't pride yourself on your Discipline right now, don't worry. The rigors and demands of property ownership, once you have committed, will quickly pull you into line out of the necessity for self-preservation, or of collapse if you don't perform.

Every project needs the final step of Delivery. The work must be finished, the drapes hung, the water system tested, the driveway paved. There will be an opening day—the first day your tenant or your purchaser comes to the site to occupy or take possession. You must be ready. The building must be opened—the ribbon must be cut. Remember the term paper that had to be handed in or the promise you made to your father to clean the garage on Saturday. This is the performance you have been rehearsing weeks and months for. The curtain must go up. People expect it.

Until it is rented or sold, no money changes hands. It must look as good as you can possibly make it. You are competing with dozens of other landlords in your market, dozens of other hotels or sellers of building lots. You want yours to be the best it can be. Pay attention to the product you are delivering. Have an opening party. Invite at least your friends. If it warrants it, invite the press and the chamber of commerce. Wellsley and Matt invited the mayor to their openings for both Courtyard and Moore Apartments. With our projects, we invited every dignitary in town we could think of. Declaring an opening day will force you to meet your self-imposed deadline for Delivery.

Desire. Drive. Discipline. Delivery. With these main principles, plus the ability to add and subtract and engage people enough to rent them one of your units, you will be able to create your own independent income in real estate whether you are building a multimillion-dollar hotel, an office building, or buying your first apartment house.

While lecturing to these very smart graduate students, I am fond of saying that each project I've acquired or built has been a miracle. In a sense, that is correct. An opportunity drops out of the sky. The money appears. Brick walls crumble. But I realize, along with Chuck, my motorcycle friend from California that things don't just happen. It takes hard work to make them happen.

And as stated in Chapter 13—A Giant Step—*As you buy your first property, and your second, and beyond, and as you continue toward your goal of creating an independent income in real estate, you will probably find, as I did, that each project tends to take on a life of its own. I used to think that business was cold, impersonal, and just numbers. Business is much more than that. Business is human interaction. You will move through your transactions step by step. You will meet brick walls along the way. If you flail away at them, they will crumble brick by brick, or you will find a way to go around them, or you will find they do not crumble, and you turn and go a different direction. As you continue on this path, you will find that the solutions often come from the people around you, from the comment that sparks an idea, from the support of a mentor or a friend that comes just at the right time to bolster your courage or bring you a solution. It is a remarkable process.*

Words and money are part of the energy that flows between us humans. It is a fascinating, satisfying, and extremely creative process. It takes courage to begin the trip. It takes courage to make the first step and to put yourself out there day after day in the process. But if you choose to do that, if you choose to borrow money, buy a property, and stay involved in the flow and the process, great wealth and happiness can come to you. If you choose not to get involved, to stay indoors, out of the fray, playing video games and watching TV—you will have a different life. Only you can know which is the right course for you to follow.

It is not that a particular project came about because I did thus and so. It is more basic than that. First comes the desire to create an independent income in real estate. From that desire, opportunities present themselves, and one then takes advantage of them. This has been my path to financial independence. You will find this too. Once you commit to purchasing a property, you will find one. But you have to be committed. You have to truly desire to own income property. The skills are basic. You have been exposed to many of them from the stories in the earlier chapters of this book.

At age twenty-three, walking down the stairs of my New York City brownstone every day, on the final flight before opening the door to face the world, I would tell myself, "There are eight million people out here in this city making a living, you can do it too!"

And so can you ...

Write down your desires. Make a list. Read it every day—*see what happens...*

ON A PERSONAL NOTE

Each of us craves certainty. We find it in the ritual of our churches, our temples, our mosques, in the common belief system and the fellowship we experience there. We find it in the sunset, on those days we can see it, and in the full moon that reappears on its twenty-eight-day schedule, and in the arms of those we love. We find it in the smiles of our friends, of our children and in arising each day to go out the door to the world of work we have found or created for ourselves. Certainty gives us a sense of security, a sense of freedom from fear.

But certainty is elusive. Some might even say it is an illusion—a necessary illusion, but one we attempt to create for ourselves in order to function in our world of friends and family, love, and work. We are bombarded with problems, politics, daily news, the sense of mayhem and crisis existing all around us. We seek shelter, security. Nothing remains the same—beliefs falter; love fails; smiles turn to grimaces of pain and suffering.

Yet somehow, we survive. We make the decisions that shape our lives. We form the relationships we need for happiness. We find the work that fulfills our need for financial security—more or less. Each of us does this in our own way.

We need information in order to make intelligent decisions. Perhaps we will never be totally certain that we are making the best choice, the best decision—but information will greatly enhance the probability that we are making the right decision for ourselves. We gather information in many ways—we study; we go to school; we talk with friends; we read on a subject; we learn all we can. But even then, information may not be enough. We didn't fall in love by getting all the information we possibly could about the person we were focused on. We don't make life-shaping decisions by simply gathering information. At some point, we have to look into ourselves. We have to see how strongly the candle is burning. Is this someone you really want to be with? Is this a path you really want to follow? Is this the job you really want to take?

At this point, a word from a friend, a prayer we offer up as a plea for assistance, a black cat in the road, or a ray of sunlight poking through a cloud can give us the sense—yes, this is what I want, or not. This is the path I want to follow. Or in the alternative—beware, wait, don't be rash. We can think through every choice rationally, but in the end, the decision of whether to venture forward or not comes from a *feeling*, or a *sense*, that this or that course of action is more likely to produce the results we want.

This book attempts to tell you my story and the story of some of the people I have guided, in the hope of inspiring you to find your own path to financial independence. Whatever path it is, it will be your own. Once you choose it, it may not be easy, but it will be inspiring; it will be your own challenge. And you will choose to face it, daily, hourly, fitting it into your current work—creating it at whatever level is comfortable for you. You may choose to keep your job for a while. You may choose to keep your job forever and simply let real estate investment be a sideline, something to augment your income.

When we make the choice to strike out on our own, it can be a frightening thing. How do we know that the decision is the correct one for us? What if we make a mistake? What if we lose everything? God forbid we should make the wrong decision.

We make a major choice in our lives when we choose to leave the security of having a boss, a supervisor, someone else to set our boundaries and direct our activities. If we choose to do it, probably we will choose to do it gradually, just as we gradually absorbed the direction and support of our parents, and step by step left home. We made a few forays into the world prior to leaving—we were walking, talking, going to school, having our first date, learning to drive the family car, but eventually we made the break—so too with our venture into real estate.

Only you can know which path is best for you, but as I have often told my own children and the students I have lectured—"If you don't choose to direct your own activities, someone else will do it for you." It took me until the age of thirty to realize the biggest lesson in life is learning to *take responsibility for your own decisions—your own actions*. No one can care for you as well as you care for yourself.

This does not mean, of course, that you should rush right out and buy a property expecting to make a fortune. It does not mean that you should leave your job. It does not mean that having a boss or a position in a shop, a school, or an organization is not the right path for you. It does mean that whatever you do in life, it is your choice—following your desires, following your heart, meeting your responsibilities, certainly—but getting in touch with what you want, whatever it is, and having the courage to follow it is the only sure way to personal success and fulfillment.

How do you get in touch with what you really want? How do you find the courage to make and follow your choices? Everyone needs to find that for themselves. For me, it has been through the practice of *Transcendental Meditation (TM®)* which has been a source of inspiration and certainty, something I most definitely needed to venture out on my own—further and further into the world of business, with all its unknown risks and rewards.

Through the process of introspection and "self-referral" which occurs spontaneously during the practice of the TM technique, I have been able to get in touch with my inmost thoughts and intuition, which has led to a sense of certainty as I moved forward.

You will find your own way, but just as I have recommended various techniques for getting in touch with your desires, techniques for finding and negotiating deals, techniques for getting yourself over the hurdle of buying your first property, I recommend the TM technique to you as a way to release the stress of business, clear your mind and get the deep rest you need to make the most evolutionary choices for yourself.

An additional resource that has helped me find a sense of certainty about which path to take, which real estate deal to pursue, which to avoid, and how to solve this or that problem, is the *Chinese Book of Wisdom*, a book some four or five thousand years old—the *I CHING*. All this may seem a bit weird to you, and perhaps it is, but several years ago, sitting in the office of one of my bankers, waiting for an appointment, I picked up a copy of *Forbes* magazine—one of the bastions of corporate thought. I don't recall the exact article, but the writer stated something to the effect that *"more and more today, Meditation and the I CHING are becoming part of the corporate board room."* I was floored. My secrets were out!

A small glimpse of the wisdom of the *I CHING* can be found in the chapter subheadings; these sayings are taken from the hexagram entitled *Limitation*, which is an excerpt from the narrative of one of the sixty-four possible hexagrams delineated in this book of oracles. It is one more tool that has been useful to me for gathering information of a kind not found on the surface in any real estate book, not found in the classroom, nor in the counsel of experts or friends. Once you have learned to use it, it can become a window into your own thoughts, your own heart, and your own internal sense of certainty, generated perhaps from your subconscious, but as strong and as infallible as anything can be in this life. At least this has been my experience, for I have sought its counsel on every project I have ever undertaken, and so far, I have never been misled.

There are a number of other books I have found inspirational. The first, of course, is a little twenty-six-page book, *It Works*. I also recommend Napoleon Hill's Think and Grow Rich, and two incredible books by Maharishi Mahesh Yogi, the very wise guru who brought TM to the West from the traditions of India: *Maharishi Mahesh Yogi on the Bhagavad-Gita* and *Silence of Being and Art of Living*.

It Works sets forth an incredible formula shared with you

throughout this book: *List your desires; read them daily; and watch life unfold.* Your desires will surely be fulfilled.

Both TM and *It Works* have something in common. Both center you on what you are and what you want from life. One of the most helpful phrases I have learned through TM is "Take it as it comes." Maharishi Mahesh Yogi gives that advice—"Take it as it comes." When you think about it, this approach applies to every situation you will ever face in life. It focuses you. It absolves you of worry. It keeps you in the moment, and it puts you in a state in which you are ready for anything. As you move forward, whether you choose to buy real estate to create your own independent income or not, keep these words in mind—"*Take it as it comes.*" You can find out more information about Transcendental Meditation online at www.TM.org.

Maharishi Mahesh Yogi once said: "*Until one is committed there is hesitation, the chance to draw back, always ineffectiveness concerning all acts of initiative (and creation).*

There is one elementary truth, the ignorance of which kills countless ideas and splendid plans: that the moment one definitely commits oneself, the providence moves too.

All sorts of things occur to help one that would never have otherwise occurred. A whole stream of events issue from the decision, raising in one's favor all manner of unforeseen incidents and meetings and material assistance, which no man could have dreamed would have come his way."
—*Maharishi Mahesh Yogi*

Mack Travis

Ithaca, NY

GENERIC PURCHASE OFFER

OFFER TO PURCHASE

_____ COUNTY

_____ of

_____ (City),

_____ (County),

_____ (State) as Buyer, hereby agrees to purchase,

and _____

of _____ (City),

_____ (County),

_____ (State), as Seller hereby agrees to sell and convey to Buyer, all of that house and lot located in Township _____, Map #_____, Block _____,

_____ (County), _____

(State), known as _____ (Street),

_____ (City),

_____ (State), for the sum of $_____

upon and subject to the following conditions:

1. The sum of $_____ as earnest money deposit shall be delivered to the Seller at the time the offer is accepted, to be held in escrow by the Seller. If the transaction is not closed, the earnest money deposit will be returned to the Buyer unless the failure to close is due to a breach of this contract by the Buyer.

2. The Buyer must be able to obtain a firm commitment by _____ (date) for loans not to exceed $_____ upon terms acceptable to the Buyer.

3. There must be no restrictions, easements, zoning, or other government regulation which would prevent the reasonable use of the real property for residential or rental purposes.

4. This offer is contingent upon the Buyer having access to the house, being able to show the house between now and the closing and securing pre-lease agreements sufficient for Buyer's needs in order to rent the property.

5. The Seller shall provide to the Buyer, at Seller's expense, a report from a licensed pest control operator stating that there is no visible evidence of wood-destroying insects.

6. The Seller agrees to leave all the window coverings, light fixtures, appliances, window air conditioners and rugs. Also, the Seller agrees to leave any furniture not desired by themselves or their family, to be specified separately.

7. *Closing shall be on or before* _____ *(date), at which time the Seller will deliver by indefeasible fee-simple title a warranty deed to Buyer subject to no encumbrances or liens, and possession of the property shall be delivered to Buyer at that time. Closing shall be at the offices of:* _____
_____.

8. *Ad valorem property taxes shall be prorated as of date of closing.*

Date: _____

Accepted:

SELLER _____

BUYER _____

SAMPLE LEASE AGREEMENT

LEASE AGREEMENT
between
[OWNER—NAME, ADDRESS & PHONE NUMBER]
and

	NAME	PERMANENT ADDRESS	PERMANENT PHONE	CELL PHONE
1				
2				
3				
4				

[Your name here], Landlord, hereby leases the house at **[Street address, City and State]** to the above named tenant(s) for a term of _____ months and _____ days commencing at 8:00 a.m. on _____ and ending at 8:00 a.m. on _____. This lease shall remain in force until the end of the term specified. The above named tenant(s) shall agree to the following lease terms:

1. To pay a rental of $_____ per month for the above house. Rent payments are to be paid monthly, in advance, and *are due the **tenth (10th)** day of each month. Please make your rent checks payable to **[Your name here]** and indicate address on the check. On group leases (with 2 or more tenants on a lease) tenants agree to pay the monthly rent in one check or in cash for all tenants on this lease. Landlord agrees to accept separate checks from each tenant for their share of the rent in the first month of the lease only. Checks may be dropped off at the office or mailed to **[Your name and address here]**.*

*2. A penalty of $5.00 per day will be charged for any rent check not received by the Landlord by the **fifteenth (15th)** day of the month for which it is due.*

*3. To pay the **last month's rent** and a **security/damage** deposit equal to one month's rent at the signing of the lease. The security/damage deposit shall be refunded in full within thirty (30) days of the end of the lease term provided there is no damage to the house and furnishings other than normal wear and that all rent and other charges have been paid in full.*

4. There is no key deposit; however, a charge of $15.00 will be made for each key issued to the tenant(s) and not returned to the Landlord by 8:00 a.m. at the end of the lease term.

5. A charge of $10.00 will be made for lock-outs after office hours (8:30–5:30 weekdays).

6. A minimum charge of $100.00 will be made should the house/room, appliances, and furnishings require cleaning by the Landlord at the end of the lease term.

7. *If the lease is executed by more than one person as tenants, all persons named shall be bound to the lease terms jointly and severally.*

8. *The tenant(s) agree to use this property as living quarters only. While it is reasonable to assume that tenant(s) will have occasional guests in their home, tenant(s) agree that there will be no large gatherings and no "keg parties" at this address at any time.*

9. *Tenant(s) must obtain the Landlord's written permission to sublet the house. The tenant(s) named in this agreement remain responsible for the terms of this lease when subletting the house/room to another party. All parties involved must sign a sublease agreement available at our office.*

10. *Anyone residing at this address must have a signed lease or sublease agreement with [Your name here] approved by the Landlord in order to live on the premises.*

11. *This lease is subordinate to all mortgages now or hereafter placed on the property.*

12. *The Landlord may terminate the lease agreement for tenant's non-payment of rent or unacceptable behavior. In this event, the security deposit shall be forfeited to the Landlord as liquidated damages.*

13. *Tenant(s) will pay for all damage to the premises and furnishings caused by themselves or their guests. Tenants agree to keep sink, lavatory drains, commodes, and sewer lines open at*

their own expense. (All drains are considered to be open and in good order if not reported in writing within five days of initial occupancy.) If any of the above become stopped up, tenant(s) agree to contact the office of **[Your name here]** *for maintenance.*

14. If tenant(s) breach this lease, their security deposit will be forfeited, they will pay the Landlord's reasonable attorney's fees, and the full amount of rent will still be owed by tenant(s).

15. At the end of the lease, any property left behind for more than five (5) days will be deemed abandoned and the landlord will not be responsible for it.

16. The utilities: water is to be paid by the Landlord; electric and gas are to be paid for by the Landlord up to a maximum of **$350.00** *per month. Tenant(s) agree to pay any amounts over the* **$350.00** *(for the combined gas and electric charges) per month with the overage equally divided among the tenants of the house.*

17. Tenant(s) are requested not to play musical instruments, radio, television, or stereo before 8:00 a.m. and after 10:00 p.m. loud enough to be heard by other tenants or neighbors of tenants. Tenant(s) agree to enter and leave the premises quietly before 8:00 a.m. and after 10:00 p.m. and request their guests to do the same so as not to disturb other tenants or the neighbors. Complaints from neighbors about noise can be reason for the termination of this lease, in which case the security deposit will be forfeited, and the tenant(s) will be required to cover all legal fees. Please respect the rights of your neighbors.

18. *Cable television and high speed Internet service will be paid for by the Landlord. While each room has a separate line and jack, telephone service is to be arranged and paid for by the tenant(s). For phone service contact the provider of your choice.*

19. *Tenant(s) are required to deposit all garbage and trash in the containers provided in the designated area and to carry the containers to the curb for pickup.* **After pickup, the containers must be removed from the curb and returned to the building.** *Tenant(s) will be required to pay any fine(s) imposed by the city for trash containers not removed from the curb. Tenant(s) will be charged for missing trash containers and for trash left outside containers. Tenant(s) are always required to keep lids on garbage cans tightly closed.*

20. *Tenants are required to maintain adequate heat to prevent freezing pipes in winter months. A thermostat setting of 50°F is sufficient to prevent damage during vacation periods.*

21. *No pets or animals of any kind shall be kept on the premises. VIOLATION OF THIS RESTRICTION WILL SUBJECT THE SECURITY DEPOSIT TO BE FORFEITED.*

22. *No waterbeds are to be used in this house.*

23. *The Landlord or his agents shall have the right to enter the premises for purposes of inspection, repair, and maintenance or to show the house as needed for rental.*

24. *The Landlord shall not be liable for any loss of tenant's property*

by theft, burglary or fire. It is recommended that tenant(s) purchase a Tenant Homeowner's Insurance Policy.

25. When you move in, smoke detectors will be operational. It is Tenant(s) responsibility to keep the smoke detectors operational at all times and to replace batteries as needed during the term of your lease. This is important for your safety.

26. If the Landlord is unable to deliver the house for occupancy at the beginning of the lease agreement for any reason, he shall not be held liable and the lease agreement shall remain in force, and the first month's rent shall not be owed until the house is ready for occupancy.

27. Tenant(s) or guests of tenant(s) are not allowed to use the roof of this building at any time. The roof can be damaged from sunbathing, moon-gazing, or walking. Any roof damage by the tenant(s) or their guests will be charged to the tenant(s).

28. The Landlord agrees to deliver the house to the tenant(s) in good condition. Tenant(s) are expected to maintain the house in good condition and are responsible for damages to it. A reasonable sum to repair any damages shall be paid to the Landlord by the tenant(s).

*29. We want the house to remain in good condition. If you have any difficulty with plumbing, appliances, windows, etc., please call **[Your phone number here]** as soon as possible so that any needed repairs can be done promptly. This is particularly important for any safety-related problems. Also, it is important that*

Tenant(s) call Landlord if water runs or drips in the sink, lavatory, commode, or any faucet. If a window does not open easily call the Landlord for assistance. If you break a window, you are responsible. Some top windows do not open.

30. The kitchen and living areas will be checked quarterly or as need for cleanliness. If cleaning is required, the Landlord will have it done and then deduct the expense equally from the security deposits of the tenants of this house.
31. Tenant(s) agree to keep all grounds around this property clean of debris at all times. This includes, but is not limited to: cans, bottles, paper products and cigarette butts. If the property is not kept clean, the Landlord will have it done and deduct the expense equally from the security deposits of the tenants of this building.

32. When there is space available in the parking lot for this property, only one car per tenant is allowed. Guests are asked to park elsewhere. A tenant who does not regularly drive or own a car does not have a parking space for guests. All vehicles must be registered and have current tags.

33. Furniture is to remain in the room where it was at the beginning of the lease unless the Landlord gives permission for it to be moved.

34. There will be a $25.00 charge for every returned check.

35. This is the entire agreement between the parties; there are no representations or agreements other than those contained herein;

changes in this lease are effective only if in writing, signed by both parties.

This lease agreement is hereby executed and entered into this

_____ day of _____, 20_____.

_____

Landlord

Tenant(s)

_____

_____

_____

APPENDIX C

FOR FURTHER READING

Berges, Steve. *Buying and Selling Apartment Buildings*. Hoboken, NJ: John Wiley & Sons, 2005.

Berges, Steve. *The Complete Guide to Investing in Rental Properties*. New York, NY: McGraw-Hill Education, 2004.

De Roos, Dolf. *Real Estate Riches*. Hoboken, NJ: John Wiley & Sons, 2004.

Irwin, Robert. *Buy, Rent, Sell*. New York, NY: McGraw-Hill Education, 2007.

McElroy, Ken. *The ABC's of Real Estate Investing*. New York, NY: Warner Business Books, 2004.

Nickerson, William. *How I Turned $1,000 into $1,000,000 (Now $5,000,000) in My Spare Time*. New York, NY: Simon & Schuster, 1958.

RHJ. *It Works*. Camarillo, CA: DeVorss Publications, 1926.

Wilhelm, Richard. *The I Ching (Book of Changes)*. Translated by Carey F. Baynes. Princeton, NJ: Princeton University Press, 1977.

ABOUT THE AUTHOR

Today, Mack Travis owns multiple millions of dollars' worth of property. He is invited to lecture at Cornell University at their world-renowned Hotel School and their Baker Program in Real Estate.

The International Profit Associates Company in Chicago recently recognized him with their Client Achievement award and invited him to speak to seven hundred of their star consultants—sharing the podium with Steve Forbes. (Forbes got twenty minutes, Travis got three.)

Travis is a founding member of Ithaca's Business Improvement District serving as president for seven years. He has also served six years as president of the board of directors of an affordable housing project for seniors, nine years on the board of the local medical center; and nine years on the board of directors of an upscale assisted living facility of 250 units, where he chaired the Property Committee. He and Carol, now married thirty-five years, continue to serve on local boards and charities and have been honored locally as "Distinguished Citizens of the Year."

Since this book was first published in 2011, he has written two others: *The Expansion of Happiness: A Common-Sense Look at the Transcendental Meditation Technique, Founded by Maharishi Mahesh Yogi*, Tadorna Press, 2014; and *Shaping A City, Ithaca New York: A Developer's Perspective*, Cornell Publishing, 2018.

www.ingramcontent.com/pod-product-compliance
Lightning Source LLC
Chambersburg PA
CBHW032116040426
42449CB00005B/160